designPOP

designPOP

LISA S. ROBERTS

Rizzoli
NEW YORK

New York · Paris · London · Milan

First published in the United States of America in 2014 by
Rizzoli International Publications, Inc.
300 Park Avenue South
New York, NY 10010
www.rizzoliusa.com

ISBN: 978-0-8478-4383-1
LCCN: 2014932012

Designed by Lisa Benn Costigan

Printed and bound in China

2014 2015 2016 2017 2018 / 10 9 8 7 6 5 4 3 2 1

FRED HUMIDIFIER
MATTI WALKER

design**POP**

DesignPOP explores game-changing design and the explosion of innovation in the twenty-first century. What is a game changer in the world of design? It could be a product that pioneers the use of new materials or a new production process. Or a new typology that alters our expectations about what something should look like. Game-changing design pushes boundaries, creating new possibilities—and ultimately products that enrich our lives.

BLOW-UP BOWL
CAMPANA BROTHERS

This generation has become accustomed to innovation. But it was the 1980s that marked the beginning of a mind-blowing design revolution. The obvious game-changing catalyst was the explosion of technology. Suddenly it played a role in every aspect of the design process from creation to manufacturing to distribution. New materials (resin, carbon fiber, high-performance plastics) and new processes (injection molding, laser-cutting, 3-D printing), allowed designers to realize their designs, formerly impossible or too expensive to produce. Designers innovated their way through roadblocks and historic boundaries. And toward the end of the twentieth century, a renaissance began unparalleled in the history of design.

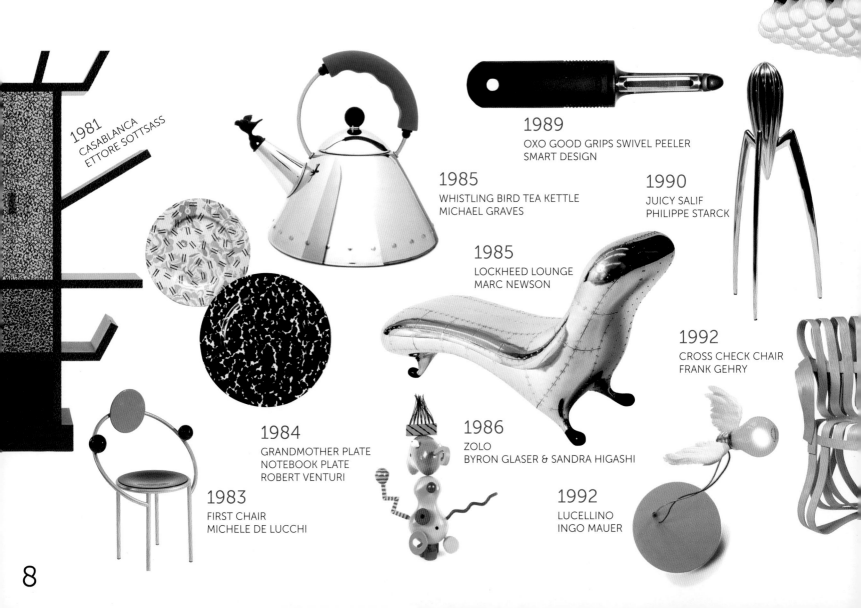

1981
CASABLANCA
ETTORE SOTTSASS

1989
OXO GOOD GRIPS SWIVEL PEELER
SMART DESIGN

1985
WHISTLING BIRD TEA KETTLE
MICHAEL GRAVES

1990
JUICY SALIF
PHILIPPE STARCK

1985
LOCKHEED LOUNGE
MARC NEWSON

1992
CROSS CHECK CHAIR
FRANK GEHRY

1984
GRANDMOTHER PLATE
NOTEBOOK PLATE
ROBERT VENTURI

1986
ZOLO
BYRON GLASER & SANDRA HIGASHI

1983
FIRST CHAIR
MICHELE DE LUCCHI

1992
LUCELLINO
INGO MAUER

Today, products need to be even more spectacular and surprising to get our attention. Materials and processes previously used only in specific industries are finding their way into consumer applications. Sustainability and social responsibility are influencing new directions. Even the definition of designer is changing as the lines between disciplines begin to blur. *DesignPOP* features a curated selection of game-changing products that have popped up since 2000. Each chapter illustrates different criteria. Taken as a whole, the breadth of ideas and innovation reveals distinct patterns in a changing industry—and hints as to how the industry might invent an even more remarkable future.

1993
85 LAMPS FOR DROOG
RODY GRAUMANS

1993
VERMELHA
CAMPANA BROTHERS

1993
MERDOLINO
STEFANO GIOVANNONI

1994
BOOKWORM
RON ARAD

1993
DYSON VACUUM CLEANER
JAMES DYSON

1994
ANNA G.
ALESSANDRO MENDINI

1995
KNOTTED CHAIR
MARCEL WANDERS

1996
GARBO
KARIM RASHID

1998
DR. SKUD
PHILIPPE STARCK

1997
EGG VASE
MARCEL WANDERS

1998
IMAC G3
JONATHAN IVE

List of Products

materiality

Designers are more inventive than ever in the ways they use materials. Aided by such resources as "material libraries," designers can look up thousands of different materials and determine what is best to use for each design. The availability of information has given designers the opportunity to be more creative. A great example is the use of Tyvek, a popular material originally produced for insulation in house construction. This synthetic paper is now being transformed into lighting fixtures, wallpaper, bags, coats, and much more. Another instance can be found in the application of epoxy resins to carbon fibers. This combination makes the delicate carbon fibers so strong and resilient that they can be woven into sturdy yet extremely lightweight chairs. These examples illustrate how increased knowledge and increased choice of materials has opened up a world of possibilities to the designer that didn't exist before.

DROR BENSHETRIT'S REGAL ARMCHAIR
PAYS HOMAGE TO THE SPREAD OF A PEACOCK'S PLUMAGE.
SURPRISINGLY, IT'S MADE OF A COMMONPLACE TEXTILE:

wool felt.

Fabricated from three sheets of heavyweight felt, the chair requires two people working simultaneously to fold the material over the minimal metal frame and secure the folds with rivets. The tight folds create dimension and provide structure, so the felt, not the frame, supports the sitter.

Benshetrit was inspired by the dual purpose of a peacock's feathers. The birds attract mates with their beauty, while their expansive wingspan defends against potential attackers. That same duality is expressed in his chair. Felt, generally a soft and cozy textile, has been rendered structural, strong, and fierce via a system of tightly folded, undulating pleats.

Peacock Chair

"I ALWAYS TRY TO SIMPLIFY METHODS OF CONSTRUCTION OR MATERIALS,"
SAYS BENSHETRIT, "AND IN THIS CASE IT WAS BY CREATING A CHAIR WITH
NO SEWING OR UPHOLSTERY INVOLVED."

DESIGNER: DROR BENSHETRIT
MANUFACTURER: CAPPELLINI
DATE: 2009
MATERIALS: FELT, POWDER-COATED STEEL
DIMENSIONS: 35.5"H x 43.25"W x 17"D

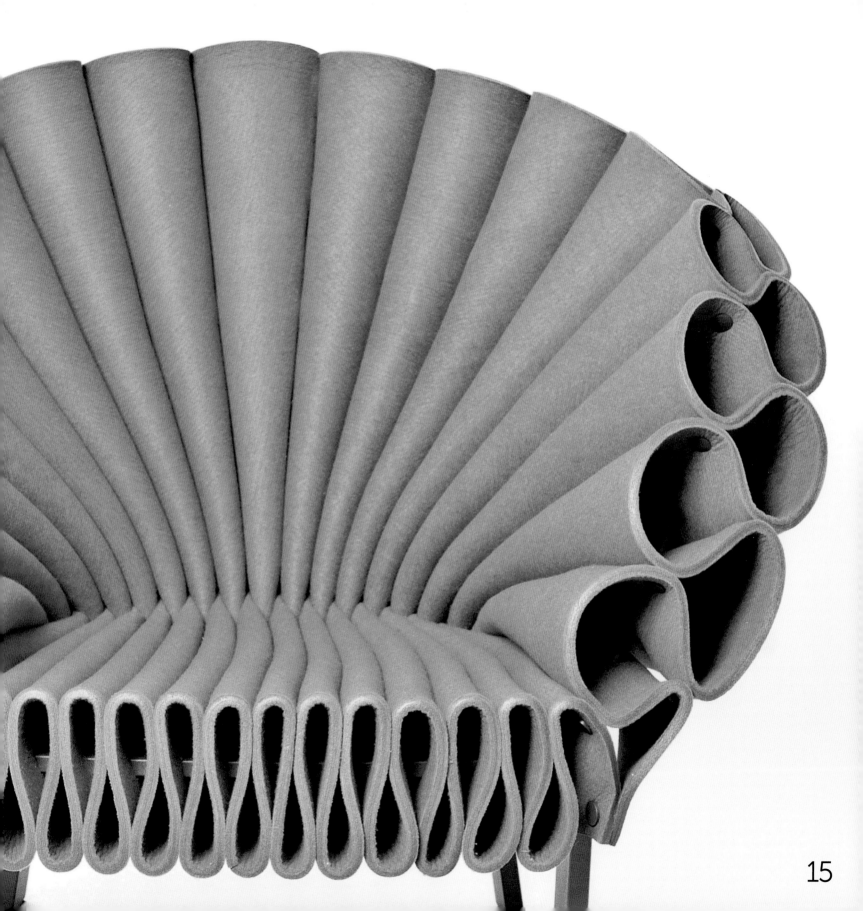

15

Soft Urn

At first glance, there's nothing unusual about the Soft Urn. It looks like the traditionally shaped classical vases made out of ceramic or earthenware. It's only when you touch the surface that you realize it's made of soft, pliable silicone rubber. Hella Jongerius has transformed an industrial substance into a beautiful object.

To make the vase, she poured liquid silicone into a mold. The mold is made in several pieces so excess material oozes through the crevices. Rather than cleaning off this excess, Jongerius leaves it there to create the unfinished edges. These raw seams—and the bumps, scratches, and bubbles on the urn's surface—lend the piece a handmade quality. They also reveal traces of the casting process and call attention to its unlikely material. Soft Urn's imperfections are the decoration on an "undecorated" vase. So is the translucence of the silicone rubber. Light glows through the vase, especially at its mouth. These are features you would never find in a ceramic vase.

FURTHERMORE:

SHOULD IT DROP ON THE FLOOR, NOT TO WORRY— IT MIGHT BOUNCE BUT IT WON'T BREAK.

DESIGNER: HELLA JONGERIUS
MANUFACTURER: JONGERIUSLAB
DATE: 1999
MATERIAL: SILICONE RUBBER
DIMENSIONS: 9.5"H x 8"DIAM

Marcel Wanders believes the future is rooted in the past. As part of a strategy he calls "lost and found innovation," the designer zeroes in on important moments in design history to "reintroduce what was almost forgotten." Here, that moment is the early 1960s, and the innovation is Achille Castiglioni's Cocoon lamps, which were abstract steel skeletons coated with sprayed fiberglass. Wanders wraps the familiar outline of a chandelier with a composite of resin and polymer fiber. It stiffens into a cocoon, producing a piece that looks like a ghostly old chandelier overrun with cobwebs. The crystal ball nestled in the center adds a shimmering effect to the softly diffused light.

Zeppelin

Of the references that inform Zeppelin, its name might be the most baffling. How is this lamp related to an airship? Wanders says he imagines the light fixture as "a miniature prototype of the most theatrical zeppelin ever to be made." He pictures it as a vessel that carries us through time and space. In the end, the designer's plan to place little figurines of people inside the crystal ball didn't stick, but he kept the name. It was one of many guiding lights. Wanders's chandelier-shaped adaptation takes us back in time, and then into an enchanted future. How totally transporting.

DESIGNER: MARCEL WANDERS
MANUFACTURER: FLOS
DATE: 2005
MATERIALS: STEEL, PMMA, CRYSTAL, SPRAY-ON-RESIN
DIMENSIONS: 29"H x 43.3"DIAM

"WE ARE SITTING TOGETHER IN THE CRYSTAL BALL,"
WANDERS EXPLAINS, "TRAVELING THE WORLD
WITHOUT A PLAN, WITHOUT A DESTINATION."

19

DESIGNERS: HUMBERTO & FERNANDO CAMPANA
MANUFACTURER: ALESSI S.P.A.
DATE: 2010
MATERIAL: BAMBOO
DIMENSIONS: 5.75"H x 25.5"DIAM

20

Blow Up
Bamboo Centerpiece

Visiting Alessi's factory, the Campana brothers saw different lengths of metal pieces lying around and got the idea to create a bowl made of "a chaotic snapshot of metal fragments emanating from a central explosion." They went back to their studio to make the prototypes. "Because we didn't have a welder at that time and it was difficult to find one, we started cutting bamboo and gluing it ourselves, attaching one piece to another to make the prototype in real scale." Alessi used the prototypes to construct the Blow Up Collection, first in stainless steel and a few years later in bamboo, the original prototype material.

THE STORY OF THE BLOW UP SERIES BEGINS AND ENDS WITH BAMBOO. THE MIDDLE IS ABOUT STAINLESS STEEL.

There's no question the bowl is beautiful in bamboo, but the segue from cold metal to warm bamboo is also symbolic. It celebrates five years of partnership between the Campanas and Alessi.

Midsummer
Light

With Midsummer Light, Tord Boontje introduced a new design vocabulary—one that melds historic decorative motifs with industrial materials and modern technology. This piece brought history forward and catalyzed a resurgence of interest in ornate detailing and themes of flora and fauna. Even more remarkable than its impact on the design world, this lush floral cascade somehow starts its life in a flat, oversize envelope.

Midsummer Light is packaged as two sheets of Tyvek, an indestructible synthetic paper that doesn't tear and is commonly used in construction as insulation. The light also comes with a flattened plastic cone that, once assembled, guides the shade's conical shape and keeps the paper from touching the bulb. Boontje made twenty full-size models to achieve the correct draping. Bootje explains "Each model was cut by hand using two days and lots of scalpel blades."

To add dimensionality, the die-cut sheets are two-toned—they are lighter and darker versions of a single color—and one sheet's leaves are smaller than the other's. The end result is complete transformation. You'd never guess this machine-made piece wasn't handmade, or that this luxurious garden was ever flat enough to slide beneath a door.

DESIGNER: TORD BOONTJE
MANUFACTURER: ARTECNICA
DATE: 2004
MATERIALS: DIE-CUT TYVEK, MYLAR CONE
DIMENSIONS: 30"H x 18"DIAM

Designing an object without worrying about how it could be made is a designer's dream. Konstantin Grcic got such an assignment when he and forty-nine others were asked to create fantasy objects in honor of the Italian manufacturer Moroso's fiftieth anniversary. To his surprise, Moroso loved Grcic's design for the bench and wanted to put it into production. The problem was finding the right material to create a structural seat. Hollow in the center, the large circular bench would collapse in the middle if made with most types of plastic. Fortunately, a new type of plastic called Hirek had just been invented. Its unique properties made it similar to the human bone, smooth on the outside and porous on the inside. It could be formed into this delicate design, with its abundance of cutouts, and still be structural.

Osorom

GRCIC NAMED THE PIECE FOR THE MANUFACTURER (OSOROM IS "MOROSO" SPELLED BACKWARD). WITHOUT THE COMPANY'S PERSEVERANCE, THE PROJECT WOULD STILL BE JUST A FANTASY.

"The search for the right material and technology normally determines a project from very early on, often triggering the design process. With Osorom, everything happened the other way round. The piece was completely designed on the computer, without consideration of how and in what material it could be made."
Konstantin Grcic

DESIGNER: KONSTANTIN GRCIC
MANUFACTURER: MOROSO
DATE: 2002
MATERIAL: HIREK PLASTIC
DIMENSIONS: 13.75"H x 47.25"DIAM

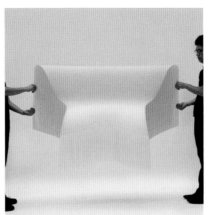

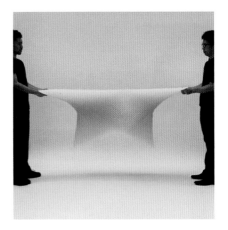

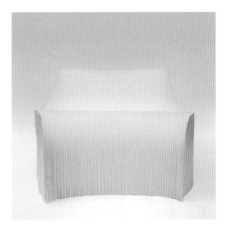

Honey-Pop

Once made,
the seat cannot be modified—
whoever's butt gets there first leaves
the lasting impression.

Have you ever tried to sit on a foldout paper party ball? Probably not. However, Japanese designer Tokujin Yoshioka used the same material and concept to create a chair in a similar fashion. The Honey-Pop chair is made from just 120 sheets of thin glassine paper. There's no metal, wood, or screws. The sheets of paper are glued together in a way that, when expanded, create a sturdy honeycomb structure. The chair arrives flat and is less than an inch thick. It is pulled open like an accordion, and then someone sits on it to form the seat. Surprisingly, when the honeycomb paper is compressed it has enough strength to support the weight of a person.

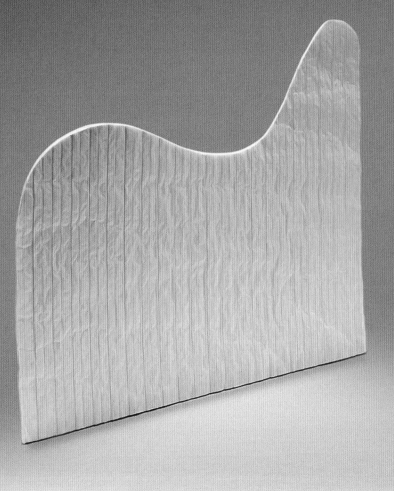

DESIGNER: TOKUJIN YOSHIOKA
MANUFACTURER: TOKUJIN YOSHIOKA
DATE: 2001
MATERIALS: PAPER
DIMENSIONS: UNFOLDED: 31.25"H X 32"W X 32"D
FOLDED: 31.25"H X 36.5"W X .75"D

27

To:Ca Clock

Turned off, it looks like a solid block of polished maple.
Turned on, bright red numerals seem to hover on its surface.

HOW DOES IT DO THAT?

The seemingly solid chunk of wood is actually made from MDF, an engineered wood product, and then covered with a very thin maple veneer. LED lights shine from within to display the time. The veneer is just thin enough, and the light is just strong enough, to strike a perfect balance between these two elements. Not too long ago, this award-winning clock would have been impossible to design. Today, with newer materials and technologies, what once seemed like magic is now pure ingenuity.

DESIGNER: KOUJI IWASAKI
MANUFACTURER: TAKUMI
DATE: 2002
MATERIALS: MDF, HARD MAPLE VENEER, LED CLOCK
DIMENSIONS: 3.5"H x 8.25"W x 3.5"D

Lighting innovator and designer Ingo Maurer views lighting design as an art form. Culling from high-tech and mundane materials, he crafts ingenious lights, such as the MaMo Nouchies—a series of lamps made out of paper. The Samurai Lamp is part of the series. The series' name is a compilation of Maurer, the lighting designer; Dagmar Mombach, the inventor of the technique that transforms the paper; and Isamu Noguchi, the legendary designer whose Akari light sculptures modernized paper lamps. But whereas Noguchi's were geometrically controlled, Maurer's renditions are sensual and organic.

Samurai Lamp

The shade begins as a plain sheet of Japanese paper that is transformed during an eight-step procedure. All done by hand, the process involves wetting the paper, binding it with thread, folding and pulling it into a complicated shape, and letting it dry. Then the paper is loosely draped over a wire frame. It appears to have the fluidity of fabric, but it also has enough rigidity to keep its shape. The true essence of the material comes through when the light is turned on. It becomes animated with an ethereal glow, almost as though the Samurai himself has come to life.

DESIGNERS: INGO MAURER & DAGMAR MOMBACH
MANUFACTURER: INGO MAURER
DATE: 1998
MATERIALS: PAPER, METAL, STAINLESS STEEL, SILICONE, GLASS, GLASS-FIBER SHADES
DIMENSIONS: 29.5"H x 31"W x 8.5"D

DESIGNER: TOKUJIN YOSHIOKA
MANUFACTURER: YAMAGIWA CORPORATION
DATE: 2000
MATERIALS: METHACRYLATE, ALUMINUM
DIMENSIONS: 11.5"H X 14.25"W X 3"D

ToFU Lamp

Most lights are made of two components—the fixture and the light source. Japanese designer Tokujin Yoshioka has successfully merged these two with his starkly simple ToFU lamp. It's a single block of pure translucent acrylic that glows when the light is turned on. Mimicking the process for making tofu, Yoshioka developed a delicate technique for pouring, setting, and slicing resin into an aluminum-clad halogen bulb that's inserted into a hole in the side. When it's turned on, light passes through the clear acrylic and highlights the four edges of the square. Ultimately, ToFU is not really a lamp in the classic sense, but an expression of light itself.

DESIGNERS: BERTJAN POT & MARCEL WANDERS
MANUFACTURER: MOOOI
DATE: 2004
MATERIALS: CARBON FIBER, EPOXY RESIN
DIMENSIONS: 40.2"H x 20.5"W x 24"D

34

Carbon Chair

CARBON FIBER IS A HIGH-TECH MATERIAL WHOSE
PROPERTIES—STRENGTH, FLEXIBILITY, AND LOW
WEIGHT—MAKE IT A NATURAL FOR THE AEROSPACE,
CIVIL ENGINEERING, AND MILITARY INDUSTRIES.
SO HOW DO YOU MAKE IT INTO A CHAIR?

Designers Bertjan Pot and Marcel Wanders are known for
taking materials out of context. To make the Carbon Chair,
they first dipped carbon fiber in epoxy resin to stabilize it.
Before the epoxy cures, the fiber is handwoven on a mold
shaped like a seat. The configuration on the seat looks
random, but it's actually a strategic "strength pattern."
The weave is denser in areas destined to bear the most
weight, and every point on the rim of the seat is connected
to the four points joining the seat to the frame. "By working
directly on the mold," says Pot, "all the strands can be woven
in the best possible way to guide forces and tensions through
the product." In a further meshing of this high-tech material
with a low-tech process, the chairs are made at a factory
in the Philippines that specializes in woven rattan.

chapter 2

Process

Laser cutting, 3-D printing, and injection molding

may sound to the uninitiated like scary torture tactics, but they are actually commonplace manufacturing processes. Newer processes are even more mind-boggling. Who has ever heard of inflating steel to create a chair, or of capturing a sneeze with a digital scanner to design a vase? Not too long ago these designs were unimaginable. Some are created specifically around the process. Others begin with an idea, and then the manufacturing technique is invented or sought out—and sometimes processes are adapted from a different industry. The game is constantly changing, and the future is clearly boundless.

Smoke Dining Chair

WAS THIS CHAIR RESCUED FROM A BURNING BUILDING?

In fact, the chair and the rest of the Smoke series grew from the designer's desire to challenge notions of beauty and perfection. "I asked myself, what actually is decoration, and why are we always striving to make it as perfect as possible?" says Maarten Baas. "I wanted to do the opposite of making it more symmetric, more perfect—I wanted to try and reverse that thought."

His first attempts involved soaking, scratching, and throwing chairs off tall buildings. He then tried and selected the blowtorch. The trick was to burn the piece just long enough so that the ashes retained their integrity. Then he injected the charred remains with clear epoxy resin. The resulting surface was surprisingly smooth considering its highly textured appearance, and the chair itself was unexpectedly solid. Baas reinforced these contrasts by using crisp and unblemished leather upholstery. The chairs are made in Indonesia, where craftsmen produce an original chair, then burn it. The designer believes burning the chairs gives them an entirely new life.

DESIGNER: MAARTEN BAAS
MANUFACTURER: MOOOI
DATE: 2002
MATERIALS: BURNT WOOD, EPOXY RESIN, LEATHER
DIMENSIONS: 42"H x 19"W x 22.5"D

Maarten Baas likens
the blowtorch to a
sculptor's chisel, with one
important difference:
"A good sculptor knows
what the chisel will do.
I feel more like I'm the
director. I come expecting
coincidences. But I am
there to say, 'NO, STOP.'"

39

Vase of Phases

Why the name **Vase of Phases?**
It refers to the transformation process—whole to broken and back
to whole again—with all the phases revealed at the same time.

This vase appears to be irrevocably broken, as if someone had cracked it with a hammer
or dropped it on the floor. And yet Vase of Phases is not broken at all. The mess of jagged
pieces is intentional. The designer Dror Benshetrit began with an intact porcelain vase and
coated its interior with silicone to hold it together when he broke it. He manipulated the
shards, and the smashed original became the mold for Vase of Phases.

The greatest challenge was figuring out how to keep the vase
somewhat intact, without it shattering to pieces. We went through
a lot of experiments before getting to the final result. Dror Benshetrit

Even the process is symbolic. Benshetrit subjects a porcelain vase—the iconic fragile object—
to a traumatic experience, and then pieces it back together. "The conspicuous damage adds
to the appeal," says Benshetrit. "It's like having a scar that reminds you of a certain moment in
life. It's a design that people instantly understand."

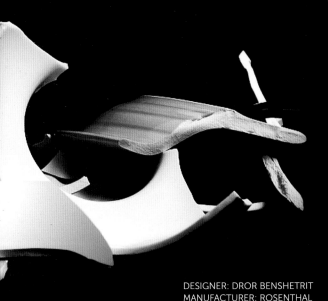

DESIGNER: DROR BENSHETRIT
MANUFACTURER: ROSENTHAL
DATE: 2005
MATERIAL: PORCELAIN
DIMENSIONS: 9.25"H x 6"W

Chippensteel Chair

The form of the Chippensteel Chair may reference the antique Chippendale style of furniture, but the similarities end there. This chair has been inflated as if it were a rubber tire. Polish designer Oskar Zieta began working on the technology for blowing up steel objects as soon as he graduated from architecture school in 2000. His goal was to expand the versatility of a cheap and common material: SHEET METAL. Zieta's tough, playful pieces are made by FiDU (free inner pressure deformation), a process adapted from the automotive industry. The designer is working on further developing the process so that consumers will one day be able to buy the pieces flat-packed and inflate them at home.

PROCESS:
The metal-inflation method begins with a laser cutter shaping a 0.5 mm sheet of steel. Then a welding robot stitches two of the sheets together to make a pocket. This robot also makes the perforations in Chippensteel's seat and back. The pocket is inflated like a silver balloon, using approximately 100 TONS OF AIR PRESSURE. Once blown up, the chair is bent into the proper angles.

DESIGNER: OSKAR ZIETA
MANUFACTURER: ZIETA PROZESSDESIGN
DATE: 2009
MATERIAL: STEEL
DIMENSIONS: 28"H x 16"W x 23.6"D

Bin Bin

Trash cans come in so many shapes, but until Bib Bin, no one ever thought of making one that looks like trash. Its function clearly inspired its form. In his pursuit for just the right crumple, designer John Brauer made hundreds of miniature paper bins, then crushed and unfolded them before hitting on one with "the perfect balance between order and chaos." The final product is made of rigid, high-density polyethylene, preserving this perfect crumple for all time.

DESIGNER: JOHN BRAUER
MANUFACTURER: ESSEY
DATE: 2004
MATERIAL: HIGH-DENSITY POLYETHYLENE
DIMENSIONS: 13.25"H x 13.25"DIAM

I think that good design remains over time. It's the opposite of fashion. Rainbow is out of the ordinary. It's magic, fun, and interactive, and how it uses light and color makes it a unique object. Patrick Norguet

Rainbow Chair

Who doesn't marvel at a rainbow? Its ethereal beauty and range of color evoke a sense of joy, and Patrick Norguet's Rainbow Chair does the same. It references this natural wonder in both its emotional lure and its deceptive simplicity. Run your finger over the surface of the chair, and you'll find it to be perfectly smooth. There are no bumps or ridges—a remarkable feat of technology.

Every color in the chair is a separate slice of acrylic resin—forty-four slices. These plates are fused together using ultrasound technology. The chair is completely transparent and allows light to pass through without interruption. Rainbows of color are cast on the surrounding floor or walls; and when the light source is sunlight, the effect grows and diminishes throughout the day. This interaction between light and color almost gives the chair a fourth dimension. One might ask, is this about form, function, or illusion? The answer would be: all three!

DESIGNER: PATRICK NORGUET
MANUFACTURER: CAPPELLINI
DATE: 2000
MATERIAL: ACRYLIC RESIN PLATES
DIMENSIONS: 31.5"H x 15.35"W x 20"D

The One Shot stool was created on a computer and built with a 3-D printer, never having been touched by human hands. 3-D printing allows designers to create things that previously would have been impossible to fabricate. Patrick Jouin, who has embraced this technology in his work, created one of the first large-scale pieces with movable parts using this process.

The design for the One Shot stool began with a simple inspiration—the three-legged wooden stool that milkmaids pick up "in one shot" and move from cow to cow. At first glance, this reimagined version with its complex seat and splayed legs appears to be made of many pieces. It's not. In fact, it's built in one piece without screws, bolts, or connectors. The stool, like its inspiration, can be picked up in one shot—pull the handle at the seat's center and the legs twist shut, so the whole thing resembles a folded umbrella. Push down and the column transforms into a complex and intricate seat. In just one fluid movement, the shape of the piece has shifted completely. Jouin went beyond designing an object. As he puts it, he "designed the gesture . . . and the gesture designed the object."

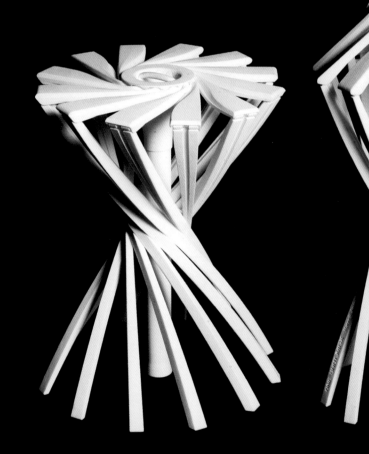

IS JOUIN A WIZARD OR IS HE THE BENEFICIARY OF SOME OTHERWORLDLY TOOLS? HAS 3-D PRINTING MADE HIM A BETTER DESIGNER?

Resolving the mechanics of the stool would have been impossible without a computer. It allowed him to develop the mathematical formulas to make the stool structural and to integrate the complex decorative elements. One Shot is the product of a beautiful marriage of wand and wizard. Tools are essential, but so is the designer who can use them to realize his dreams.

DESIGNER: PATRICK JOUIN
MANUFACTURER: .MGX BY MATERIALISE
DATE: 2006
MATERIAL: POLYAMIDE
SIZE: 15.75"H x 12.5"DIAM OPEN; 25.8"H x 4"DIAM CLOSED

One Shot Stool

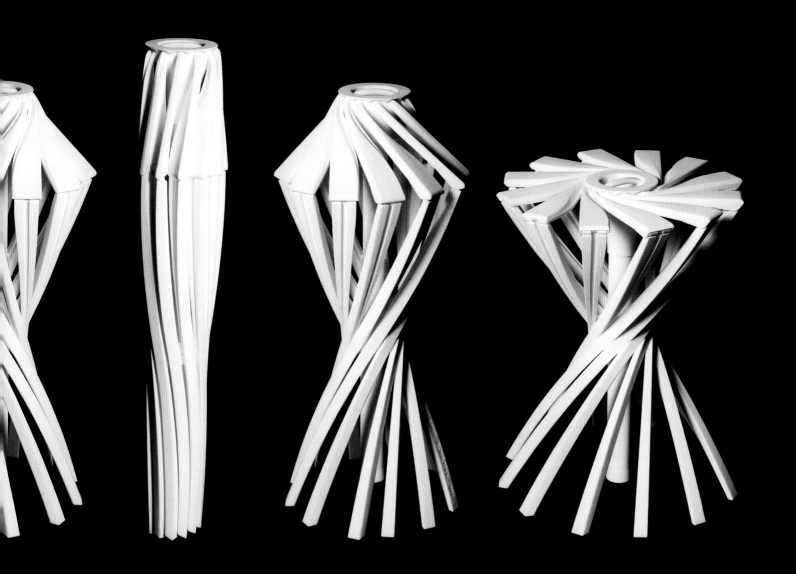

Crevasse

DESIGNER: ZAHA HADID
MANUFACTURER: ALESSI
DATE: 2005
MATERIAL: 18/10 STAINLESS STEEL
DIMENSIONS: 16"H x 3"W x 2"D

Zaha Hadid is world-renowned for her mind-bending architecture and is the first woman to win the Pritzker Prize—the architectural equivalent of the Nobel Prize. Her first built project didn't happen until her mid-forties. Less than twenty years later her firm became one of the most successful in the world, with 950 projects in 44 countries and 300 employees. As with many architects, Hadid transferred her design vocabulary to a smaller scale to create furniture and furnishings.

Crevasse is one of her most affordable projects. Like her buildings, the stainless-steel vase pushes boundaries by experimenting with a new spatial concept. Three of its surfaces are flat. The fourth torques— its top and bottom turn in opposite directions.

Connecting this twisted side to the rest of the vase is an incredible feat of manufacturing. The unembellished design leaves no room for error. When arranged in pairs, so that all of the sides can be seen at once, the vases resemble architecture more than their actual purpose. So, who needs flowers?

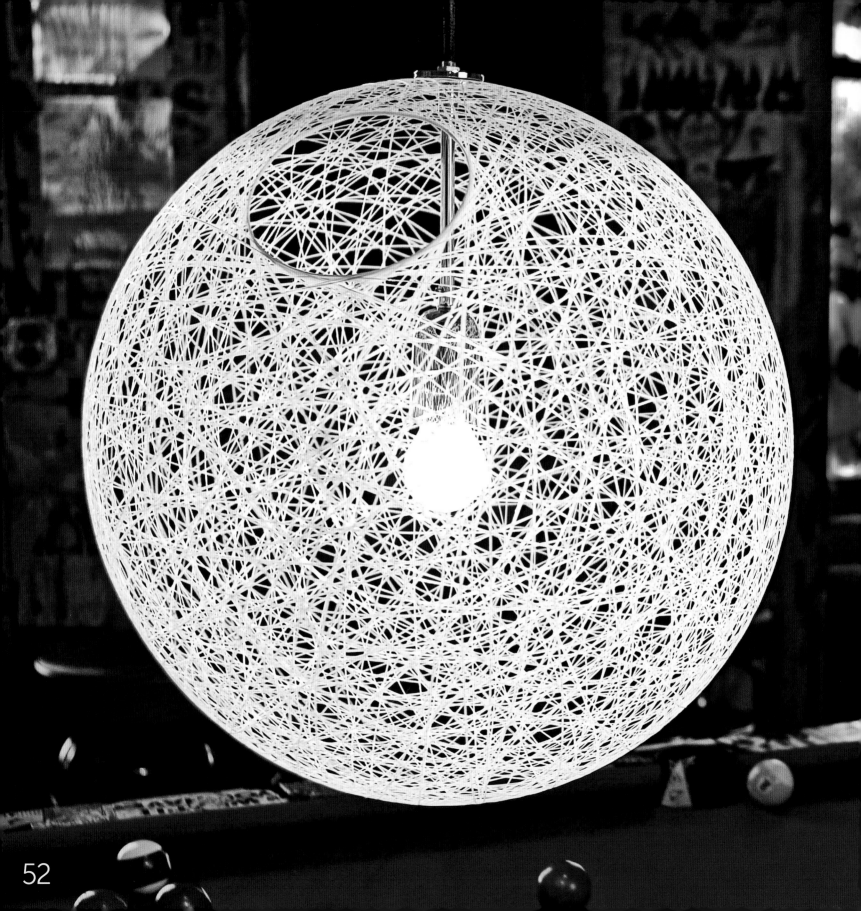

The process for making the Random Light took designer Bertjan Pot three years to develop. Understandably, he's keeping his process close to home. There have been many attempts to copy it, but none compare to the original.

Random Light

THE PROCESS BEGINS WITH EPOXY-DIPPED FIBERGLASS STRANDS THAT ARE COILED AROUND AN INFLATABLE BEACH BALL. WHEN THE EPOXY HARDENS, THE BALL IS DEFLATED AND EXTRACTED.

As Pot says, "The skin becomes the product." Like the Carbon Chair (in the previous chapter), the pattern may look random but is actually a carefully calculated design. The pattern covers the ball completely and consistently. The hole at the orb's top is crucial to the lamp's functionality—this is where the light bulb is inserted and changed. Pot's top-secret process allows a soft textile to become rigid, and a large airy sphere made of string to be self-supporting, structurally sound, and positively ethereal. When the glass fibers diffuse the light from the exposed bulb, the whole thing glows and casts its pattern across the ceiling and surrounding walls.

DESIGNER: BERTJAN POT
MANUFACTURER: MOOOI
DATE: 2001
MATERIALS: FIBERGLASS SOAKED IN EPOXY RESIN, CHROMED-STEEL PENDANT
DIMENSIONS: 31.5"DIAM

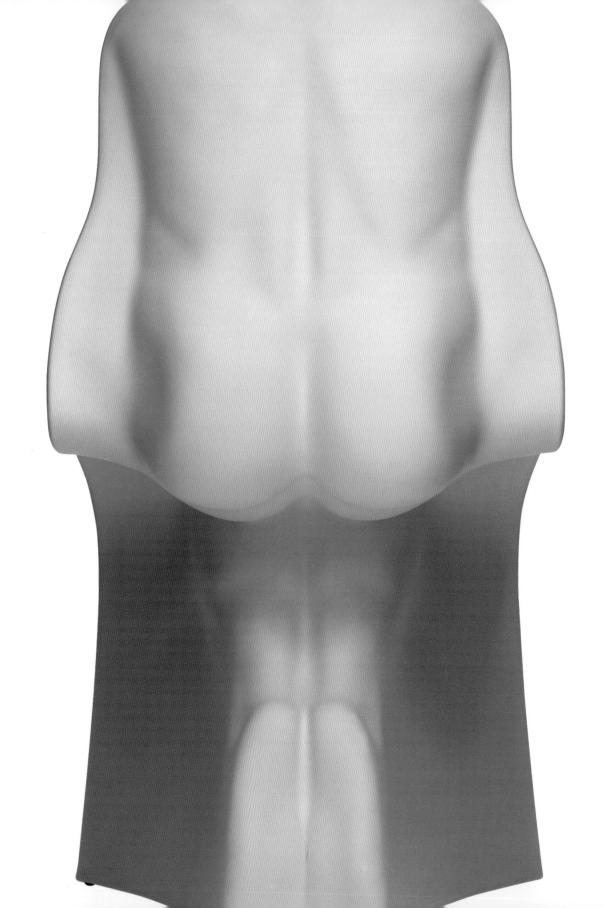

54

Him & Her Chairs

Created by Fabio Novembre, the agent provocateur of design, the chairs' alluring silhouettes of naked bodies make for tantalizing seats. Discussing his chairs, Novembre quotes from the Book of Genesis as it relates the creation of Adam and Eve. **Him** (born of the earth) and Her (born of his rib) felt no shame in their nakedness. With such perfect bodies, is it any wonder?

The bare derrieres are crafted using techniques that range from old school to high tech. The chairs began as plaster sculptures, and through a variety of advanced technologies (three-dimensional scanning, rotational molding), the final products are plastic replicas of the human body, perfectly shaped to hold yours.

DESIGNER: FABIO NOVEMBRE
MANUFACTURER: CASAMANIA
DATE: 2008
MATERIALS: POLYETHYLENE
DIMENSIONS: 34.25"H X 19.5"W X 24"D

Illusion Side Table

Illusion is the perfect name for John Brauer's amazing, gravity-defying side table, which appears to drape like a tablecloth without the support of a table. Here's an object no passerby can readily comprehend. It prompts the question: Is this for real? The designer got the idea while walking past a Copenhagen café where servers were preparing for lunch. There were round tables with white tablecloths. Each cloth was square and almost touched the floor. "I stopped and took a photo through the window with my phone," he says. "I wanted to freeze that image." He took the photo to a plastic workshop and asked if it was possible to reproduce such an object. They said no, but Brauer persisted and invented a process in which a worker takes a sheet of acrylic softened in an oven, drapes it over a form, and hand-manipulates the material to sculpt folds. Though each Illusion table is slightly different, all share the four points that make contact with the ground to provide support. "It was not easy to make a 3 to 4 mm acrylic/PMMA sheet act as a 0.5 mm tablecloth," say Brauer. The designer was tenacious about finding the right material and process to make it possible to fool his audience.

DESIGNER: JOHN BRAUER
MANUFACTURER: ESSEY
DATE: 2006
MATERIALS: ACRYLIC/PMMA
DIMENSIONS: 18"H x 16"DIAM

Blossom

Elena Manferdini designed an elegant fruit bowl for manufacturer Alessi, but it lived on the shelf for several years before they found a process to mass-produce it. Blossom is more complex than it looks.

It was determined that stainless steel would give the right support; and laser cutting, with its minute precision, was the right process to transform the notion of ornamental pattern into structure. It was also the right process and material to realize the design's remarkable complexity.

DESIGNER: ELENA MANFERDINI
MANUFACTURER: ALESSI
DATE: 2011
MATERIAL: STAINLESS STEEL
DIMENSIONS: 8"H x 8"W x 8"D

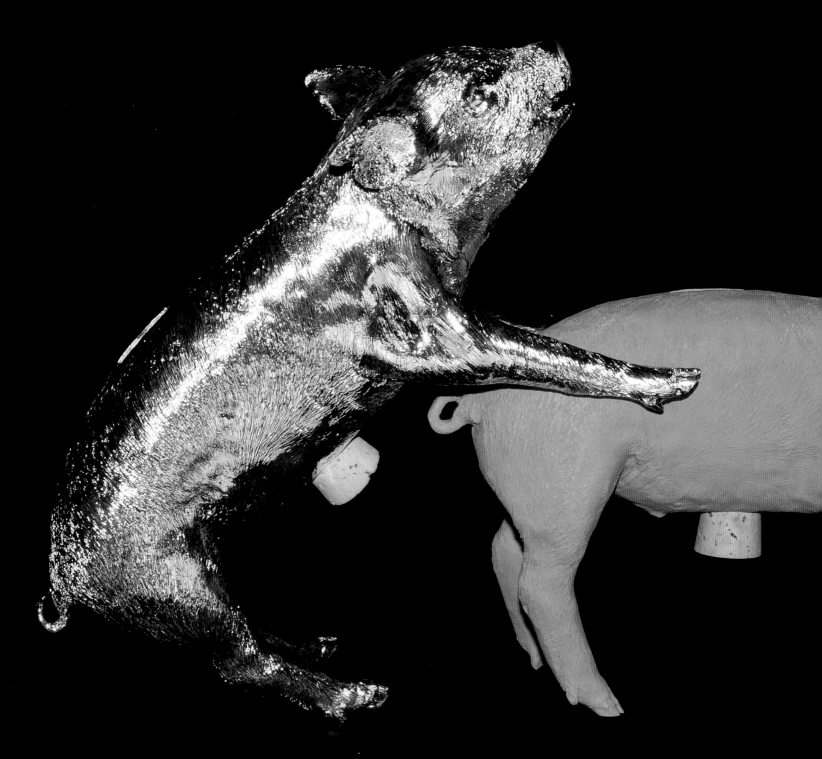

Bank in the Form of a Pig

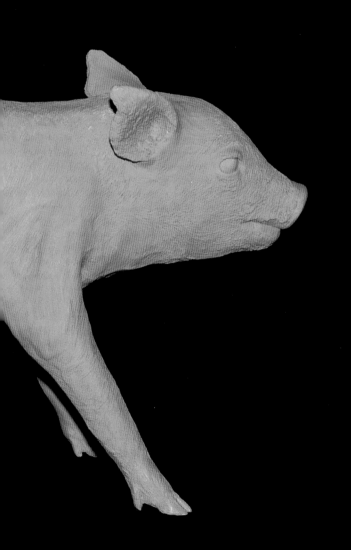

SOMETIMES I LABOR OVER
DESIGNS. THIS ONE WAS JUST
AN AHA MOMENT: WHAT IF I
MADE A PIGGY BANK THAT
ACTUALLY LOOKS LIKE A PIG?
HARRY ALLEN

Designers often look to reality for inspiration. Harry Allen
went one step further with Bank in the Form of a Pig,
using a real piglet as his model. Allen is quick to point
out that no animals were harmed in the process—the
pig had already died of natural causes. After being
stuffed by a taxidermist, it was sent to a museum-quality
caster. He created a highly detailed silicone rubber mold
that articulated every hair and every wrinkle. A cast of
the pig was made with polyester resin and pulverized
marble, giving it heft and exquisite detailing. Just so no
one is confused as to what this pig is for, Allen plugs its
underbelly with an oversized cork.

DESIGNER: HARRY ALLEN
MANUFACTURER: AREAWARE
DATE: 2004
MATERIALS: CAST POLYESTER RESIN, CHROME FINISH, CORK
DIMENSIONS: 10"H x 5.25"W x 18"L

Chubby Chair

3-D PRINTING HAS BEEN AROUND FOR ALMOST THIRTY YEARS.

It's now entering the next generation, getting faster, cheaper, and capable of creating large-scale objects. Dirk Vander Kooij is on the forefront of this revolution. He was the first to develop a way to make large objects using the extrusion process. Vander Kooij repurposed and reprogrammed an out-of-work robot to extrude melted plastic recycled from old refrigerators. The multi-axis robot can lay down material in various dimensions and colors.

For the Chubby Chair, the molten plastic is extruded into shape and then cooled in a mold to create the form. The legs and seat are separate pieces that are bolted together. The whole process takes just a few hours. The thick lines made by the extruded plastic exaggerate the texture inherent in most 3-D printing processes. This low resolution becomes part of the beauty of the chair, looking as if it were squeezed straight out of a tube of paint.

Until now 3-D printed furniture was priced like art (in the $1000s) and had to be treated as such. But the Chubby Chairs (in the $100s) would be a "no brainer" to have around your breakfast table.

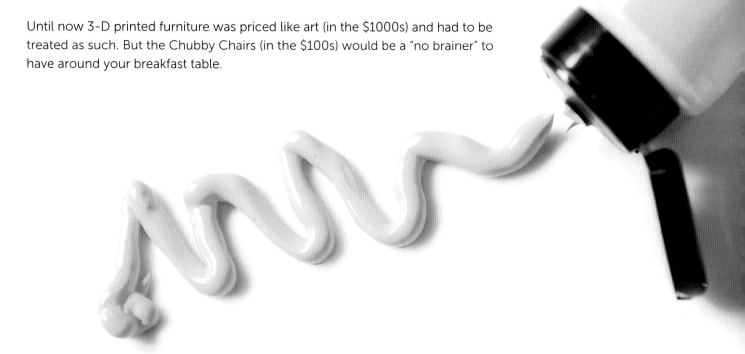

DESIGNER: DIRK VANDER KOOIJ
MANUFACTURER: STUDIO VANDER KOOIJ
DATE: 2012
MATERIALS: PLASTIC (RECYCLED REFRIGERATORS)
DIMENSIONS: 31.5"H X 16.5"W X 18.5"D

design for
technology

A product needs to function admirably to be considered good design. Some designers take products that have been around for a lifetime and decipher how to enhance their functionality. Companies like OXO and Joseph Joseph do this with household and kitchen tools. They don't reinvent old products or even invent new products—they improve existing ones. Adaptability is another hallmark of functionality: Is the product relevant and useful in many different situations? New technologies have upped the ante. Previous generations of designers were not fielding commissions for computers, cell phones, digital clocks, smart phones, or MP3 players. What should these look like, and how should their design support their functionality without getting in the way? The products that endure are the ones that are more than just a pretty, sleek, or fancy face.

James Dyson's impact on the household appliance industry has been nothing short of revolutionary. As inventor, designer, and engineer, he changes not only the look of these objects but totally redesigns their technologies. He is perhaps best known for his Dual Cyclone series of vacuum cleaners—the first bagless vacs with bright colors, easy attachments, and incredible sucking power. Next came the Airblade, the superfast, high-powered commercial hand driers found in public bathrooms. Now, he has reimagined the common household desk fan and created an entirely new typology.

Dyson Air Multiplier

The Dyson Air Multiplier is the first-ever bladeless fan. A small electric motor in the base of the unit draws in air and pumps it up and out through a slit inside the ring. Air travels around the ring and is propelled into the room. Without blades that chop the air, the fan's airflow is smooth, powerful, and consistent.

With each generation his products evolve, improving and expanding their functionality. Up next on his hit list: the portable heater.

DESIGNER: JAMES DYSON
MANUFACTURER: DYSON
DATE: 2009
MATERIALS: ABS, POLYCARBONATE MATERIALS
DIMENSIONS: 19.53"H x 12"W x 5.98"D

Unlike any of its predecessors, Creature transformed all expectations as to what a set of speakers should resemble. Industrial designer Kurt Solland was given the assignment to create a small cube-shaped speaker, but he ignored it as too "inside the box." Rather, he drew on his background as a sculptor and created this sensual and anthropomorphic form that looks quite alien, with a nod to Darth Vader.

Every functional element of the speakers has been fully integrated into the design. Two bullet-shaped knobs on the larger unit (the subwoofer) control the bass and treble. Small round buttons on one speaker are touch sensors for volume control. There is even a green light that glows under each speaker when the power is on, adding to their alien allure.

Though Creature's introduction in 2000 marked a turning point in audio design, it didn't happen in a vacuum. Just two years earlier Apple had released its egg-shaped iMac, encased in blue translucent plastic. It wasn't long before the iMacs had these Creatures to keep them company.

DESIGNER: KURT SOLLAND
MANUFACTURER: HARMON MULTIMEDIA, JBL BRAND
DATE: 2000
MATERIALS: PLASTIC, METAL
DIMENSIONS: SUBWOOFER 10"H x 9"W x 9"D,
SPEAKERS 3"H x 3"W x 3"D

Creature

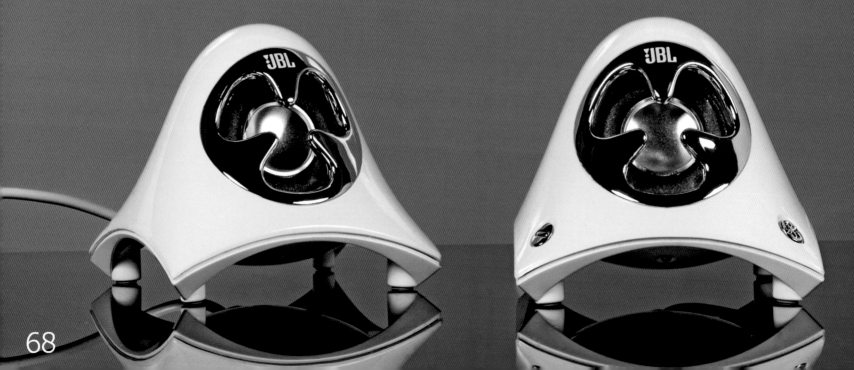

iPhone

Over 420 million sold, and counting . . . !

DESIGNER: JONATHAN IVE/APPLE
MANUFACTURER: APPLE
DATE: ORIGINAL 2007; IPHONE 4S 2011
MATERIALS: GLASS, METAL, PLASTIC
DIMENSIONS: 4.5"H x 2.31"W x .37"D

When Steve Jobs gave his signature keynote speech in 2007, he told the audience he was releasing three new products: "a widescreen iPod with touch controls, a revolutionary mobile phone, and a breakthrough Internet communicator." He then introduced the iPhone.

Even at first glance the iPhone was different. Most smart phones at the time had small screens and tiny keyboards. The iPhone introduced a multitouch screen and virtual keyboard. Your fingers became the stylus.

In its first six years, there were seven generations. Each one added new features: a high-definition camera with video capability; Siri, the talking "intelligent personal assistant"; a front-facing camera for video calls (and taking selfies); iCloud, which connects your phone to all your other Apple devices; and Touch ID, the futuristic fingerprint identity sensor built into the home button. By the time this text goes to print, there will probably be a new generation available with new and improved features. And within in a few years, it might just be called the iDoEverything.

Nest Learning Thermostat

NEST IS THE MOST ELEGANT THERMOSTAT YOU WILL EVER SEE. Of course that is not saying much when you think of those ubiquitous beige versions that have gone largely unchanged since the 1970s. The homely updated programmable thermostats most of us own today were actually designed to empower homeowners to conserve energy. But some of us have never even programmed them! They were just too complex. Not Nest—it's as simple to operate as it appears.

DESIGNER: BOULD DESIGN + NEST DESIGNERS: TONY FADELL, BEN FILSON
MANUFACTURER: NEST LABS
DATE: 2011
MATERIALS: STAINLESS STEEL, GLASS, LCD DISPLAY
DIMENSIONS: 1.26"H X 3.2"DIA

The device learns your daily cooling and heating habits and programs itself accordingly. The more you use it, the more it learns. The interface is bold and graphic—no more squinting to read inscrutable text and digits. The screen glows blue when Nest is cooling and red when it is heating. A little green leaf appears when it is saving energy.

Interacting with Nest is wonderfully intuitive—a stainless steel outer ring is the manual control for changing temperature. It moves smoothly, with just enough resistance to indicate functionality. It even connects to your wireless network so that you can program it remotely on your computer, phone, or tablet. Nest's designers seem to have thought of everything. But with such a remarkable innovation gap, there was everything to think of.

Looksoflat Lamp

It's no easy task to cast new light on a classic, especially one as iconic as the Luxo L-1 balanced-arm lamp, designed in 1937 by Jac Jacobsen. If anyone could do it, it's Ingo Maurer's studio. The designer is well-known for his humorous takes on tradition. Looksoflat seems familiar, making you wonder why it would be in the line of such an inventive design firm. Then you walk around the lamp and encounter its surprise. The lamp's thickness is just barely over a quarter of an inch! It's as if the original lamp has been flattened into a shadow of itself. The designer of Looksoflat was able to achieve this clever reinterpretation due to new technology. The light source, a strip of light-emitting diodes (LED), is tiny compared to incandescent bulbs. Looksoflat may look more like a prop than a proper lamp, but this sliver of a light functions as well as its predecessor. It emits a glow that's warm and bright. The joints articulate, and the arms balance to allow users to direct the light source any which way they want.

DESIGNER: STEFAN GEISBAUER
MANUFACTURER: INGO MAURER
DATE: 2010
MATERIALS: ALUMINUM, LED
DIMENSIONS: 27.5"H MAX x .31"D x 9"DIAM AT BASE

75

Jambox is not just another pretty face in the sea of electronic gadgets: it is the first intelligent, wireless speaker. Like all intelligent beings, it can learn and communicate. The speaker comes with software that can be continually updated, and the user can download apps to customize its functions. Depending on your settings, a voice (male or female, you choose) materializes to tell you when batteries are low or when an event on your calendar is near.

The tiny speaker delivers an impressively dynamic range, including a thumping bass—a quality that could only be coaxed from large speakers until Jambox's innovative engineering came along. It switches as needed from playing music to acting as a two-way speaker for phone conversations and conference calls.

Speaking of pretty faces, Jambox's skin is beautifully patterned. It's made of a single sheet of perforated steel that wraps around the inner components and is capped top and bottom with rubber. There are a multitude of color and pattern choices creating more than a hundred combinations. Now, the only decision left is which handsome face you might be taking home tonight?

Jambox

DESIGNER: YVES BÉHAR/FUSEPROJECT
MANUFACTURER: JAWBONE
DATE: 2010
MATERIALS: STAINLESS STEEL, RUBBER
DIMENSIONS: 1.5"H X 5.9"W X 1.6"D

Even before it was launched, Amiigo leapt to the front of the rapidly expanding segment of wearable technology designed to help people track their personal fitness and health data.

Amiigo

It promises to deliver the most accurate and user-friendly experience. "Promises" because, as of this writing, the product was still in development, but Amiigo's creators had already pre-sold more than five thousand units through a crowdsourcing campaign. This method of bringing a product to market has democratized the process and accelerated the speed at which entrepreneurs out-invent each other.

But back to that leap: While other personal trackers require you to punch in data after you eat or work out, Amiigo uses gesture recognition, sensor technology, and machine-learning algorithms to clock each motion as it occurs. Its two devices—a bracelet and shoe clip—are programmed to recognize more than one hundred types of exercise. If Amiigo isn't already familiar with an activity, you can teach it by setting it to "record" your gestures. It weighs all that data against physiological information (heart rate, skin temperature) to analyze how hard you are working and how many calories you have burned.

Amiigo is also a social creature. Its users can compare—and compete over—squats, laps, and reps in real time. Even as technology has pulled apart our ability to interact with each other, it is redeeming itself by finding ways to bring us back together. Amiigo's designers are smart to humanize their device by making it irresistible to such a highly instinctive aspect of human nature.

DESIGNER: AMIIGO
MANUFACTURER: AMIIGO
DATE: 2013
MATERIALS: VARIOUS
DIMENSIONS: VARIOUS

Jawdropping technologies need designers who can translate their value into appealing, intuitive products. A device is not persuasive if its learning curve is too high. When a brand-new technology is trying to compete in an already crowded consumer market, the stakes are even higher. The Lytro light field camera is an example of a product that has handled this beautifully.

When you focus a traditional camera, it captures a fixed amount of light. Lytro captures the total light field, recording the color, intensity, and direction of each ray bouncing around a space. There's no need to focus the camera, and the resulting "living image" can be endlessly edited to shift perspective, refocus, or to make it 3-D.

This concept had been around for a century, but Ren Ng figured out how to adapt the technology for consumer use while he was a graduate student at Stanford University. Forbes Magazine called light-field technology "maybe the biggest leap in photography since the shift from film to digital." Lytro's physical form celebrates this leap. The technology demanded a long lens, and the designers resolved this with a tube-like shape that looks more like a small telescope than a camera. On the opposite end of the lens is an interactive touch screen, similar to the interface on a smart phone. It required an interdisciplinary group of scientists, engineers, industrial designers and interaction designers to bring all of the elements of the Lytro into focus. 'Design for technology' is clearly a team sport.

DESIGNER: NEW DEAL DESIGN
MANUFACTURER: LYTRO
DATE: 2012
MATERIALS: ANODIZED ALUMINUM, RUBBER
DIMENSIONS: 1.61"H X 1.61"W X 4.41"D

Lytro
Light Field Camera

2013
BEST EMERGING TECH AWARD
International Consumer Electronics Show

CubeX Trio

The 3-D printer's inevitable transition from industrial to personal use is often compared to the personal computer and its dramatic shift from object of curiosity to the object none-of-us-can-live-without. Since the 1980s, when 3-D printing technology got underway, these printers have lived mostly in the realm of manufacturing. The sleekly designed CubeX is intended to fit in at home. With its smooth casing and familiar form, it wouldn't look out of place next to your kitchen coffeemaker or your home office's 2-D printer.

While many of its predecessors necessitated soldering equipment for home assembly and the know-how to program on an open source network, CubeX comes preassembled and with a database of ready-to-print designs. The machine is the first of its kind to print three colors at once (hence the name "Trio"). Its three print heads extrude heated plastic, layer by layer, to create three-dimensional objects. (Imagine a trio of mini hot-glue guns working in concert). The plastics, either PLA (a compostable corn plastic) or ABS (a very common plastic), are available in a range of eighteen colors.

As when personal computers first became personal, the impetus for investing in a 3-D printer for the household still seems a bit murky. It is difficult for anyone without an industrial design or engineering degree to imagine printing an action figure for their child or a custom case for their smart phone. CubeX's approachable design makes it a forerunner in the race to tip consumers toward embracing a new and intimidating technology.

DESIGNER: 3D SYSTEMS
MANUFACTURER: 3D SYSTEMS
DATE: 2013
MATERIALS: MULTIPLE
DIMENSIONS: 23.5"H X 20.25"W X 20.25"D

chapter 4

ShapeShifters

Question everything…assume nothing. Guided by this mantra, designers have begun to rethink the form and function of the most mundane objects. In 1990, Philippe Starck shocked us with his Juicy Salif (page 8). He challenged the conventional look of a lemon juicer and designed an enigmatic object in the shape of a stylized squid. Its success opened the floodgates for designers to question and reevaluate preconceived notions about the way things should look or work. Some of their questions are simple: Why do rarely used kitchen items have to take up so much space? Some are unexpected: Can we change the way something as basic as a dresser operates? Others seem downright implausible: Do the legs of a table need to be rigid to hold it up? There are no right or wrong answers, but there are plenty of surprising ones.

Org

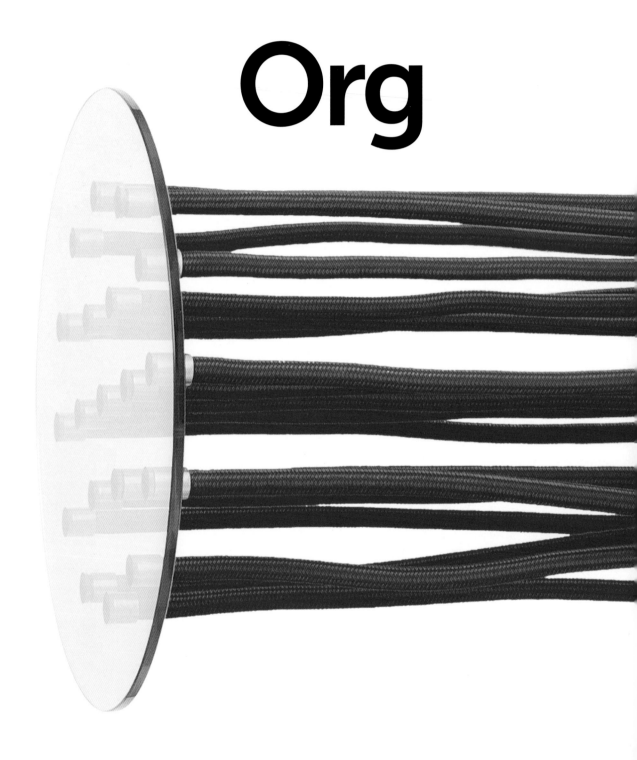

Using his talents as both an architect and a designer, Fabio Novembre has created a most unusual table that defies immediate understanding. **Org** seems to float mysteriously just above the floor on its tentacles. In fact, **Org** is quite grounded. Fifteen of the legs are loose, but four are rigid. Embedded inside these four polypropylene ropes are sinewy steel inserts that mimic the organic quality of the other free-flowing legs. A classic Novembre design, the **Org** table is sensual and tactile. It's hard not to grasp those appealing legs. Now how many tables can make that claim?

DESIGNER: FABIO NOVEMBRE
MANUFACTURER: CAPPELLINI
DATE: 2001
MATERIALS: GLASS, STEEL, POLYPROPYLENE ROPE
DIMENSIONS: 43.3"H x 23.6"DIAM

ONE SIDE IS MING.
THE OTHER SIDE IS ME.

Cédric Ragot

French designer Cédric Ragot has captured five hundred years of history with the design of his **Fast Vase**. One side, the quiet side, pays homage to ancient Chinese Ming vases. The other side is abstract and futuristic, and based on a digital image of acceleration. The designer wanted to create a sense of speed that totally contrasted with "an object that is as static in its use and expression as a Ming vase."

Fast Vase tells a dramatic story about something that is simple and recognizable, while it simultaneously impels us into the future. The subtext of the story is the impact of digital technology on our culture. Ragot refers to it as "the quantum leap that human production has known through the digital age." This vase may reveal the past and the future, but together the two sides shape the present.

DESIGNER: CÉDRIC RAGOT
MANUFACTURER: ROSENTHAL
DATE: 2007
MATERIAL: PORCELAIN
DIMENSIONS: 10.5"H

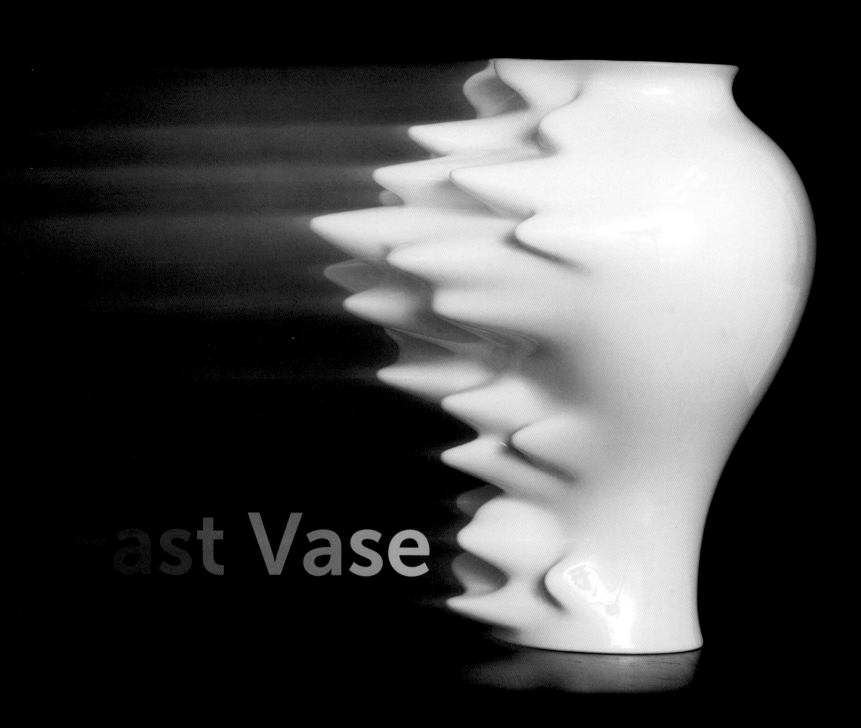

ast Vase

90

PlusMinusZero Humidifier

When applied to design, the Zen principal of *kanso*—simplicity or the elimination of clutter—can result in the total transformation of a product. That's the case with the PlusMinusZero Humidifier. It bears no resemblance to its clunky predecessors and gives no hint as to what it actually is. Japanese designer Naoto Fukasawa applied his signature minimalist approach when completely rethinking this conventional appliance. The power of his design is its absolute simplicity. Inspired by a drop of water, it's perfectly round and smooth. Only when the top half of the "doughnut" is lifted off does PlusMinusZero reveal the flawlessly designed inner workings of a functional humidifier.

DESIGNER: NAOTO FUKASAWA
MANUFACTURER: PLUSMINUSZERO [+/-0]
DATE: 2003
MATERIALS: POLYPROPYLENE, POLYCARBONATE
DIMENSIONS: 6.1"H x 12"DIAM

MARTIN STADLER, CEO OF STADLER FORM:
The design comes from a designer who does not have any technical or product design background.

MATTI WALKER:
That's why turning this shape into a well-working product was the biggest challenge we had!

Fred Humidifier

Fred is the offspring of a highly effective collaboration between the manufacturer Stadler Form and the Swiss graphic designer Matti Walker. A company that creates appliances is not necessarily going to excel at artistry; and the learning curve is high for a graphic designer who knows little about mechanical engineering. Yet together they created something successful and totally original. The emotional connection to Fred is immediate due to his anthropomorphic features—the three little feet, spherical body, and projecting snout. Cleverly designed, each feature plays a functional role. The feet elevate the unit and provide structural support. The simple, graphic body encases and reflects the minimal inner workings. And the long spout propels the steam. Humidifiers generally have a negative association—they're brought out for wintertime colds and dry air. That's not the case with Fred, whose appeal is so enduring he often ends up staying in the room, even in the off-season.

DESIGNER: MATTI WALKER
MANUFACTURER: STADLER FORM
DATE: 1999
MATERIALS: PLASTIC, CHROME-PLATED ZINC
DIMENSIONS: 10.5"H x 14.3"DIAM

Stack

Stack looks more like a work of art than a chest of drawers. The designers stripped a dresser down to its basic elements—frame, runners, and drawers—and reassembled the pieces to create a new paradigm for a piece of furniture that isn't known for inspiring reinvention. Usually, drawers are supported by an outside box frame and can only be opened in one direction. Here, an interior steel frame provides vertical support, passing through the midpoint of each drawer and allowing them all to move from side to side. If you're feeling organized, they can be lined up perfectly straight. But if you're late getting dressed, you can leave the drawers every which way and they look even better.

THERE'S A KEY ADVANTAGE TO THE MULTIPLE COLORS: besides their aesthetic appeal, they remind you what's inside— socks in the red drawer, unmentionables in the orange one.

DESIGNERS: YAEL MER & SHAY ALKALAY/
RAW EDGES DESIGN STUDIO
MANUFACTURER: ESTABLISHED & SONS
DATE: 2008
MATERIALS: BIRCH PLY, FIBERBOARD, STEEL
DIMENSIONS: 70"H x 22.2"W x 24"D

95

Tripod Trivet

Most trivets are heavy, flat objects, hidden away in a drawer when not in use. Gabriele Chiave was not satisfied with that direction. He totally changed the typology of this utilitarian pot supporter, transforming it into what looks like an elegant piece of jewelry. Aside from its unlikely form, Tripod's unique characteristic is its adjustability—the four facets can be positioned to hold hot dishes of multiple shapes and sizes. And when it's not on the table holding hot pots, it can attractively dangle from a kitchen hook. Tripod is a clever combination of function and decoration, so much so that you might even be tempted to wear it around your neck.

DESIGNER: GABRIELE CHIAVE
MANUFACTURER: ALESSI
DATE: 2007
MATERIAL: CHROME-PLATED ZAMAK
DIMENSIONS: EACH 1.25" x 1.25"; CORD 23.75"L

TRIPOD IS HARDLY RECOGNIZABLE AS A TRIVET.
IT'S A TOTAL MYSTERY UNTIL YOU REALIZE HOW IT WORKS.
THEN THERE IS THAT AHA MOMENT—A SENSE OF DELIGHT
IN THE ORIGINALITY OF A DESIGN THAT DOESN'T
COMPROMISE FUNCTION BUT INSTEAD ENHANCES IT.

Stitch

The Stitch chair folds up to a package just 15 millimeters deep (a little over half an inch). This is so skinny that twenty-five folded chairs can fit inside the space occupied by a single unfolded one. Adam Goodrum accomplished this feat by engineering a new way to collapse a folding chair. Pick it up from the center, and it closes side to side rather than front to back. When the chair is shut, it becomes completely flat.

Goodrum uses flat pieces of heavy-gauge aluminum that are connected with simple hinges. He highlights the hinges with different colored panels. This interlacing of colors becomes a key component of the design.

The Stitch chair looks and feels different—its slim profile when folded belies how sturdy it is when opened. Goodrum has truly reinvented every aspect of the conventional, and generally quite boring, folding chair.

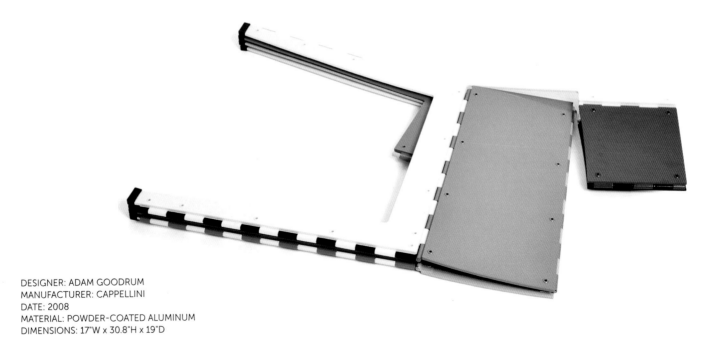

DESIGNER: ADAM GOODRUM
MANUFACTURER: CAPPELLINI
DATE: 2008
MATERIAL: POWDER-COATED ALUMINUM
DIMENSIONS: 17"W x 30.8"H x 19"D

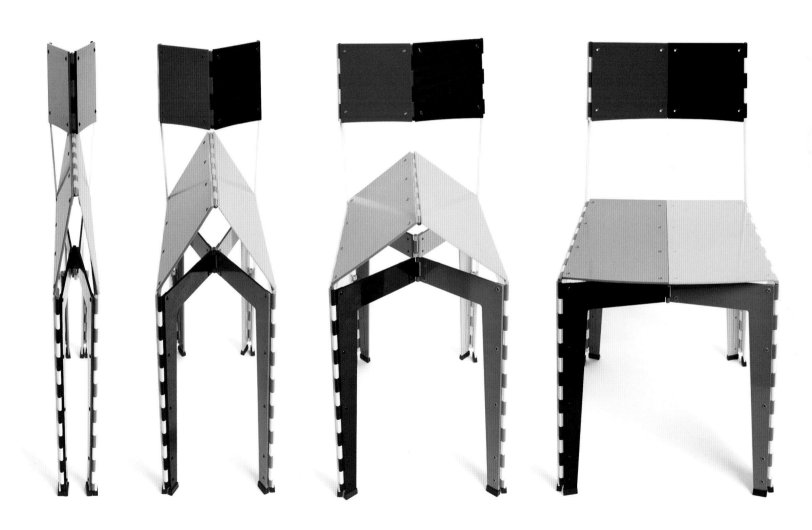

99

Garlic Rocker

Without its title, the Garlic Rocker would be unrecognizable as a garlic press.
Most of these are two-handled instruments that squeeze together to crush the garlic.

THE ROCKER ON THE OTHER HAND...ROCKS!

Just place it over the clove, press down, and rock. The crushed garlic is easily and evenly
extruded through the holes. A major headache of most garlic presses is cleanup. This is
not an issue here. The Garlic Rocker is a one-piece design with no hinges or crevices to
trap bits of garlic. Plus, it is made of stainless steel so when rubbed between the hands
under water, it removes the odiferous and often tenacious garlic smell from the fingers.

DESIGNER: GOODWIN HARTSHORN
MANUFACTURER: JOSEPH JOSEPH
DATE: 2010
MATERIAL: STAINLESS STEEL
DIMENSIONS: 7.3"L X 1.6"W X 1.2"D

I usually design products by analyzing
my basic needs.
I get my inspiration by asking myself:
Why do I not have this item in my household?

Boje Estermann

DESIGNER: BOJE ESTERMANN
MANUFACTURER: NORMANN COPENHAGEN
DATE: 2004
MATERIALS: SANTOPRENE RUBBER, STEEL
DIMENSIONS: 9"DIAM x 5"H

Collapsible Strainer

The typical kitchen colander takes up way too much space. This premise inspired Danish designer Boje Estermann to create his award-winning Collapsible Strainer, which folds into itself for easy storage and pops back up as needed. Estermann was able to create this category-changing design because of the properties of Santoprene rubber, a material that is flexible enough to fold, rigid enough to maintain its shape, capable of withstanding extreme temperatures, and sturdy enough to handle a pound of wet noodles. The designer even thought to contour the strainer's ridges so there are no hidden grooves—in its collapsed state, water reaches every inch. That means tiny pieces of food can't get stuck in the grooves, since every surface is washable. Like most phenomenal designs, the Collapsible Strainer has many imitators, but none is as good as the original.

DESIGNERS: DOUWE JACOBS & TOM SCHOUTEN
MANUFACTURER: FLUX
DATE: 2010
MATERIAL: POLYPROPYLENE
DIMENSIONS: 24.4"W x 33.5"H x 25.2"D

104

The name Flux

was chosen for its reference to a state of
constant change or flowing movement.
It also fits the definition of "flexible luxury,"
given that the suppleness of the material
gives the chair its particular comfort.

Flux Chair

The Flux Chair arrives looking like a large folded envelope with a handle. Release the flaps, bend
them around, tuck them into place, and the result is a super-futuristic form that can support up to
350 pounds. Opening the chair for the first time may require some extra force since the plastic is stiff.
But after dismantling and reassembling it several times, the plastic softens and can be assembled in
under five seconds. This makes Flux great transient furniture—easy to store and easy to transport.

The Dutch duo behind the design created the chair for their college graduation project. Their goal
was to create a ready-to-assemble chair using a single sheet of polypropylene, with no added parts
or fasteners. After working on several hundred small-scale models and then a hundred more full-
size prototypes, they achieved the perfect shape. This may be the next generation of the folding
chair—where a single sheet makes a structural seat.

Mercury Ceiling Light

Designer Ross Lovegrove, known as "Captain Organic," is driven by three things: design, nature, and art (DNA as Lovegrove likes to refer to it.) His ceiling chandelier resembles drops of silvery-white liquid mercury. Ten pods of varying sizes hang from an aluminum disk—and cleverly disguise the fact that only two of them actually contain lightbulbs. Their material is another surprise—the pods are made of molded thermoplastic with a polished chrome finish. The lightweight plastic allows them to float. The two illuminated pods shine upward and bounce off all the reflective surfaces, making it impossible to detect the original light sources. The result is an ethereal glow. During the day, the fixture functions as sculpture. Capturing natural light and the surrounding environment in its shiny surfaces, it becomes a work of art. Whether the light is on or off, the piece is strikingly futuristic. It both honors and elevates its quicksilver DNA.

WHAT NATURE DOES IS TO LIBERATE FORM;

IT TAKES AWAY ANYTHING EXTRANEOUS. THAT'S WHAT I DO.

I MAKE ORGANIC THINGS THAT ARE ESSENTIAL.

Ross Lovegrove

DESIGNER: ROSS LOVEGROVE
MANUFACTURER: ARTEMIDE
DATE: 2008
MATERIALS: THERMOPLASTIC, ALUMINUM, STEEL
DIMENSIONS: 24"H x 43.3"DIAM

variance

By its very definition, mass production creates clones. A steady march of lookalikes into the marketplace has created a hunger for variation. Designers are meeting that demand with strategies to introduce differences from one mass-produced piece to the next. One strategy is to incorporate some element of unpredictability during the stages of manufacturing; another is to design an object that can be assembled in different ways; and a third technique is to engineer the production process so that some part of it is made by hand. The ultimate goal: humanizing mass production.

Nobody's
Perfect Chair

Done in this way,
you don't have copies
of an object, but originals.
Just as people have a
right to be different,
objects also have a
right to be different.

Gaetano Pesce

Most objects made of plastic have perfect, uniform shapes. The Nobody's Perfect chairs take a different direction. Italian architect and designer Gaetano Pesce developed a production process that builds in variability so that no two pieces are exactly alike. An artisan pours liquid resin into a mold, adding colored pigments as he goes. The way the resin spreads throughout the mold and the movement of the colors vary from chair to chair, expressing the individual preferences of the maker. Each of the chairs is unique and somewhat imperfect. The designer considers them creations, birthed at the hands of the individual artisans. So it isn't any wonder that each even comes with its own birth certificate.

DESIGNER: GAETANO PESCE
MANUFACTURER: QUATTROCCHIO
DATE: 2002
MATERIALS: POLYURETHANE-BASED RESIN, NYLON PINS
DIMENSIONS: 37.4"H x 16.3"W x 16.3"D

A click, a peg.
We used the most advanced technology so that these elements can be assembled by hand, forgetting that their exact connections were manufactured with microscopic rigor.
Ronan & Erwan Bouroullec

Algues

Algues (French for "algae") is a single piece of plastic that can be assembled in infinite configurations. The algae-like pieces are connected with pegs to create a decorative wall frieze or a free-hanging screen. Add more twigs for opacity—for a fully seaweed-y look—or take pieces away for a lacy effect. The algae even cast shadows on the floor or wall, adding another layer of intricacy.

The repetition of a single motif is an aspect of both nature and technology—think of a blade of grass or a pixel. Algues is an elegant coupling of these notions. The identical parts are mass-produced, but the results can be as varied as trees, snowflakes, or sheaves of seaweed. It's up to the user to become the designer and to make, with very little effort, his or her own masterpiece. Establishing nineteen points of connection on each piece was a complicated endeavor, but it ensured that no two assemblages would be alike. In fact, it would be almost impossible to replicate one with another. Mass-produced AND one of a kind—voila!

DESIGNERS: RONAN & ERWAN BOUROULLEC
MANUFACTURER: VITRA
DATE: 2004
MATERIAL: INJECTED POLYAMIDE
DIMENSIONS: EACH PIECE 12.25"H x 10"W x 0.5"D

113

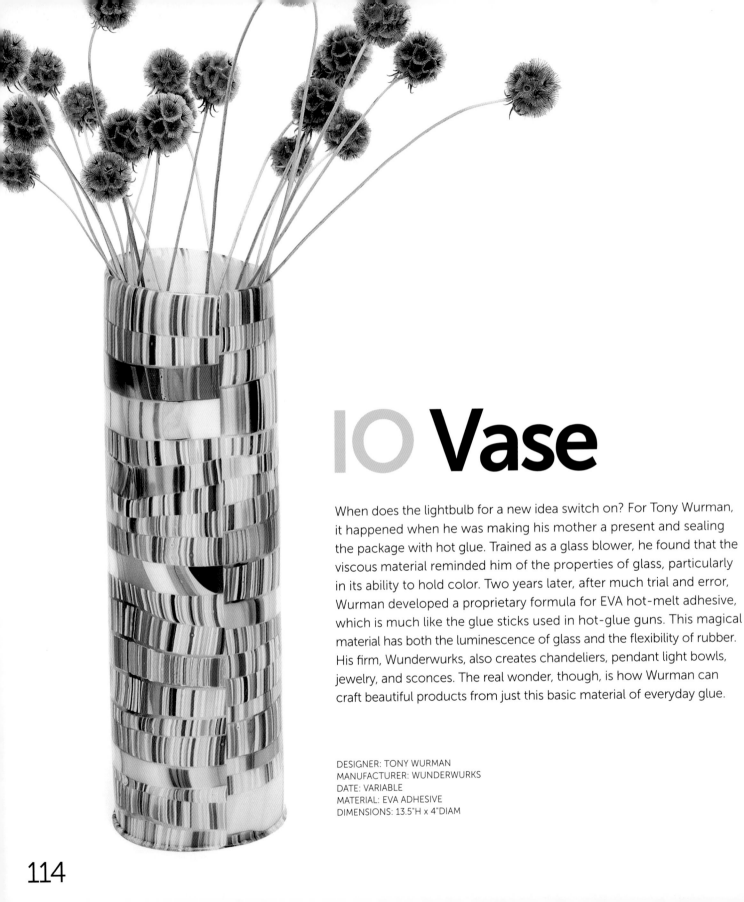

IO **Vase**

When does the lightbulb for a new idea switch on? For Tony Wurman, it happened when he was making his mother a present and sealing the package with hot glue. Trained as a glass blower, he found that the viscous material reminded him of the properties of glass, particularly in its ability to hold color. Two years later, after much trial and error, Wurman developed a proprietary formula for EVA hot-melt adhesive, which is much like the glue sticks used in hot-glue guns. This magical material has both the luminescence of glass and the flexibility of rubber. His firm, Wunderwurks, also creates chandeliers, pendant light bowls, jewelry, and sconces. The real wonder, though, is how Wurman can craft beautiful products from just this basic material of everyday glue.

DESIGNER: TONY WURMAN
MANUFACTURER: WUNDERWURKS
DATE: VARIABLE
MATERIAL: EVA ADHESIVE
DIMENSIONS: 13.5"H x 4"DIAM

115

Vase #44

Imagine creating a design just by using the sound of your voice. Digital designer François Brument developed a process that utilizes 3-D modeling techniques to transform vocal reverberations into shapes. The project is called Vase #44, and each set of sounds produces a unique vase. The version here was created by the words "David, I Love You."

Each "voice-crafted" vase is totally unique, but since it's produced by a 3-D printing process, the exact vase can be duplicated innumerable times. Therefore, it's possible for any and all of you who love a David (or not!) to own a "David, I Love You."

HOW DOES IT WORK?

First you speak))) into the computer's microphone ⚲, and then a digital image of a vase appears onscreen 🖥. Each word combination or intonation yields a differently shaped vase Ⓜ. The longer you speak, the taller the vase; the louder you speak, the wider the vase. You have sixteen chances to create a shape you like. Then you select one of the images, and that file is sent to a 3-D printer. A month later, the finished vase shows up at your front door ✉.

DESIGNER: FRANÇOIS BRUMENT
MANUFACTURER: LUMINAIRE WITH 3D SYSTEMS
DATE: 2010
MATERIAL: SLS POLYAMIDE
DIMENSIONS: 8"H x 13"W x 8.5"D (AS PICTURED)

To be continued

IT IS A TRANSFER OF THE DECISION-MAKING PROCESS FROM
"HOW TO DESIGN A DEFINITE OBJECT" TO
"HOW TO MAKE A RECIPE THAT DESIGNS OBJECTS."
Julien Carretero

DESIGNER: JULIEN CARRETERO
MANUFACTURER: JULIEN CARRETERO
DATE: 2008
MATERIAL: POLYURETHANE COMPOSITE
DIMENSIONS: APPROX 34.5"H x 73"W x 32"D

Julien Carretero developed his interest in unpredictability within mass production while studying design in the Netherlands. His thesis, *Theme and Variation*, evolved into an unusual series aptly named

To be continued…

He found a way to use a repetitive system of construction that produces variety rather than consistency. Applying this process to the design of a bench, he constructs it in layers, with each one different and influencing the next. The piece is made vertically, lying on its flat side. The designer hand-pours an expanding foam composite into a rigid mold to make the first "slice." For each consecutive slice the same composite is hand-poured into a flexible mold. The bench grows taller and taller, gradually mutating as each layer is slightly less perfect than the one before. The nature of the material, gravity, and human error take over. Carretero compares the process to a game of "whisper down the lane," in which what is being said is slightly modified along the way. All the benches start out the same, but no two finish alike. The form of each evolves at the individual moment of creation so that, in essence, the bench designs itself.

Airborne Snotty Vase

Ah-choo! The Snotty Vase may look like a delicate, hand-sculpted vase, but it's actually the physical manifestation of those nasty particles that spray out during a sneeze. The form represents a single mucus or spittle micron, enlarged a thousand times.

HOW DOES THE DESIGNER GIVE SHAPE TO SOMETHING THAT IS OTHERWISE INVISIBLE?
For each of the individual versions of the vase, an individual sneezes into a three-dimensional scanner (GROSS), which takes a digital image of the microscopic specks (GROSSER). The image is transferred to a computer, on which a designer enlarges one of the specks and manipulates it, adding a hole for a flower. The final vase is then brought to life using a 3-D printer (in a process similar to that used for the One Shot stool).

Three-dimensional printing is what inspired Wanders to create this simultaneously attractive and revolting design. "One of the important new ideas about the technique is the complete absence of molds and so the complete freedom of form," he says. "I wanted to create a [shape] we had never seen before." Clearly, he's succeeded!

DESIGNER: MARCEL WANDERS
MANUFACTURER: MARCEL WANDERS STUDIO
DATE: 2001
MATERIAL: SLS POLYAMIDE
DIMENSIONS: 6"H x 6"W x 6"D

Do hit Chair

Every Do hit Chair starts the same—as a welded stainless steel cube—and every Do hit Chair ends up differently as a customized seat for your particular bottom. The cube arrives "to be assembled," accompanied by a sledgehammer. When you whack it into shape, you become the co-designer. A video of designer Marijn van der Poll reveals his process: hit, sit, hit, sit until you find the perfect fit.

Van der Poll was drawn to the contradiction between craftsmanship and mass production. The steel cube is eminently reproducible. It only becomes a unique object once it's hammered, pounded, and dented (earplugs recommended!).

DESIGNER: MARIJN VAN DER POLL
MANUFACTURER: DROOG
DATE: 1999
MATERIALS: STAINLESS STEEL, HAMMER INCLUDED
DIMENSIONS: 27.5"H X 39"W X 29.5"D

▶ cut-up, dyed, and glued

◀ straight out of the box

Fontessa
Shoes for Melissa

Gaetano Pesce's Fontessa shoes start as ankle boots. They're constructed of plastic droplets that are intended to be cut away. Possible outcomes include a sling back, peep toe, flip-flop, ballet flat, or even loafers. Snip and paint the remaining circles your favorite color. Be-ribbon, be-dazzle, paint ladybugs, add buttons—the only limit is your ingenuity. Fontessa is a collaboration between you and Gaetano Pesce, an internationally renowned designer who has surrendered creative control. How often in life is that going to happen?

DESIGNER: GAETANO PESCE
MANUFACTURER: FONTESSA SHOES FOR MELISSA
DATE: 2010
MATERIALS: MELFLEX, 100% RECYCLED PLASTIC
DIMENSIONS: VARIABLE

If you have a hard time making decisions, this might not be the piece for you. Showtime Multileg Cabinet offers

16 DIFFERENT LEG STYLES

with the intent for you to mix and match. The body of the cabinet is simple and unadorned. There's no hardware or extraneous detail to distract you from the real drama—those cartoonish giant legs. Which to choose: historic, contemporary, or fantasy? Select one of each—or make them all the same. The idea is to make it your own.

Showtime
Multileg Cabinet

DESIGNER: JAIME HAYON
MANUFACTURER: BD BARCELONA
DATE: 2006
MATERIALS: LACQUERED MDF, ALDER WOOD
DIMENSIONS: 52"H x 39"W x 20.5"D

chapter 6

blurring the lines

Is it design, art, or craft? This assessment is increasingly harder to make as boundaries between these categories are blurring. Traditional definitions state that "design" refers to functional, mass-produced products; paintings and sculptures are "fine art" with little or no functional purpose; and "craft" denotes handmade objects with varying degrees of utility. These classifications don't take into account new developments, such as artists mass-producing their creations, designers incorporating variability into their production processes, and craftspeople finding ways to produce handmade items in multiples. Just to further confound debates over where to slot an object, there are also collaborations. Designers, artists, craftspeople, and even fashion designers are working together to produce objects that are hybrids. Clothing as chair upholstery, furniture as painter's canvas, and candle as sculpture . . . what next?!

WrongWoods Sideboard

Furniture designer Sebastian Wrong partnered with artist Richard Woods to create their WrongWoods series of furniture. Wrong's simple, unadorned sideboard makes a great canvas for the oversize and stylized wood-grain paintings that Woods generally sells in art galleries.

The collaboration is one in a series engineered by Established & Sons, where Wrong acts as design director. He based this cabinet's design on DIY plywood-furniture patterns from post-WWII Britain. The form and construction are intentionally straightforward.

Each piece is printed using wood blocks and enamel paint. Inside and out, the sideboard's plywood surfaces are covered with Woods's artistic interpretation of the material.

DESIGNERS: SEBASTIAN WRONG & RICHARD WOODS
MANUFACTURER: ESTABLISHED & SONS
DATE: 2007
MATERIALS: PLYWOOD, WOODBLOCK PRINTS
DIMENSIONS: 25.25"H x 102.5"W x 16"D

"IT'S MASS-PRODUCED AND ALSO HANDMADE,"
SAYS WOODS. "TO ME, IT'S MORE INTERESTING
THAN SELLING PRINTS IN A GALLERY."

The unusual collaboration between Ron Arad, architect and furniture designer, and the fashion house of Issey Miyake effectively blurs the line between furniture and fashion. First, there was Arad's Ripple Chair, whose striated texture suggested ripples left in the sand by retreating waves. Arad, a friend and fan of Issey Miyake, saw parallels between his chair and Miyake's signature pleated clothing.

A-POC, an acronym for A Piece of Cloth, is a computer-driven manufacturing process developed by Miyake with design engineer Dai Fujiwara. A computer-programmed loom produces an entire garment in one fell swoop, eliminating the need for hand-sewing and piecework. Arad was attracted to the technology and its potential to eradicate exploitation. "Working for the furniture industry and researching upholstery, I saw rows and rows of sewing machines and sweatshops," he says. "I thought, why can't we harness A-POC's knowledge and inventiveness to our field as well?" The opportunity to connect the two unlikely pieces became obvious when the designers realized the chair's "infinity" shape allowed for armholes. As upholstery, the textile covers the chair, providing a comfortable cushioned seat. When it's removed, it transforms into a wearable vest or "piece of cloth."

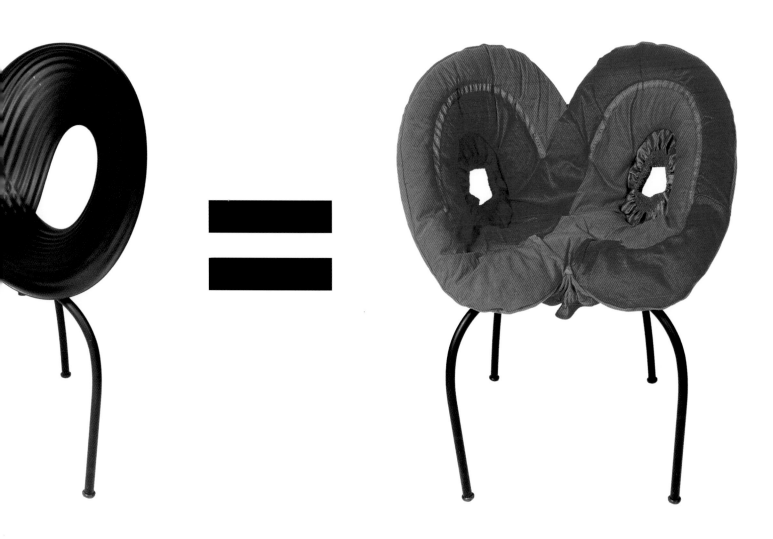

Ripple Chair + A-POC Gemini Vest

RIPPLE CHAIR
DESIGNER: RON ARAD
MANUFACTURER: MOROSO
DATE: 2005
MATERIALS: POLYPROPYLENE, STEEL
DIMENSIONS: 31"H x 27"W x 24"D

A-POC GEMINI VEST
DESIGNERS: ISSEY MIYAKE & DAI FUJIWARA
MANUFACTURER: A-POC
DATE: 2006
MATERIALS: WOOL, COTTON, DOWN
DIMENSIONS: VARIABLE

Love Bowl

Designer Stephen Burks is at the forefront of the cultural fusion movement, collaborating with non-Western cultures to create design for the western world. With his **Love** Bowl, that partnership influenced all aspects of the finished product—materials, manufacture, function, and aesthetics.

In 2005, Burks traveled to Cape Town, South Africa, to work with artisans as part of the Italian manufacturer Cappellini's socially responsible **Love** line. He developed a reverse slip-casting technique using recycled glass tiles and liquid silicone. Both of these materials are inexpensive and readily available. The process begins by placing a bowl upside down and coating it with a layer of silicone. Glass tiles are then hand-positioned into the silicone in concentric rings. A second layer of silicone is added on top.

When the silicone dries, the vessel becomes flexible and wobbly. Its appearance is reminiscent of stained glass, but both the binding and the tiles are translucent. As with stained glass, there's a narrative embedded in the **Love** Bowl: neither the artisans nor Burks could have come up with this unusual process on their own. It's a true fusion of Western design thinking and low-tech, indigenous craft techniques.

DESIGNER: STEPHEN BURKS
MANUFACTURER: CAPPELLINI S.P.A.
DATE: 2005
MATERIALS: GLASS TILES, SILICONE
DIMENSIONS: 7.5"H x 16"DIAM

I'm not one to say, "Save the planet." I'm more interested in saving people.

Stephen Burks

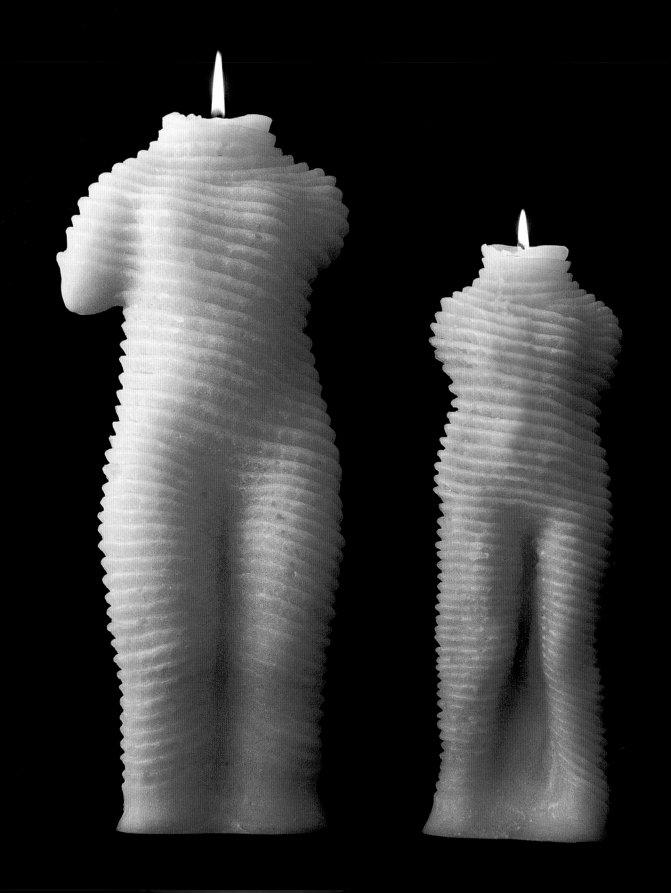

Rados

Acclaimed artist Michele Oka Doner instilled the Rados candles with her sense of spirituality. When lit, the flames burn slowly down the center and the figures glow from within.

Doner is best known for her large-scale public art exhibitions inspired by the natural world. *A Walk on the Beach* at the Miami International Airport consists of two and a half miles of terrazzo floor embedded with bronze sea creatures. Another famous piece is her silver Christofle vase, shaped like a curled palm frond.

She typically sculpts her creations in wax before casting them in precious metals. For these candles, the wax form itself became the finished product. The designs are reminiscent of her figurative sculptures made of bronze. "The figurative candle was a fresh approach to the vertical candle," she says. "I wanted to create something that was both timeless and yet contemporary. A classic."

Though the candles are mass-produced and identical, each ebbs in its own unique way; and, as in life, they yield plenty of enjoyment in the process. Perhaps that's why Oka Doner named the candles "Rados," from the Serbian word *radost*, or happiness.

> THE RADOS CANDLES ARE MORE THAN THE SUM OF THEIR PARTS. WHAT IS HOPEFULLY OMNIPRESENT IS THE GLOW OF A FIGURE IMBUED WITH FLAME. OUR LIFE IS LIKE THAT FIGURE BURNING.
>
> Michele Oka Doner

DESIGNER: MICHELE OKA DONER
MANUFACTURER: CERABELLA, SPAIN
DATE: 1997
MATERIAL: PARAFFIN WAX
DIMENSIONS: 13"H / 15"H

Zig Zag
Shoes and Bag

The Brazilian company Melissa has been producing "jelly" shoes, worn around the world, since 1979. For its twenty-fifth anniversary, the company asked Humberto and Fernando Campana to design a variation of their signature shoe. For inspiration the brothers looked to one of their previous designs, the Zig Zag screen designed in 1995. "The screen was an investigation into the idea of letting a line flow freely, without rigidity. We were trying to deconstruct the process of weaving."

The design vocabulary is pure Campana brothers. They are known for ordered chaos, overlapping of lines, and deriving inspiration from their native country and its designed environment. The original 1995 screen had been inspired by the sight of tangled hoses lying in a yard in São Paolo. The Zig Zag shoes and bag were their first forays into fashion. "The act of making a shoe brought us closer to our public, transforming this poetry [the art of weaving] into something more accessible," said Humberto Campana.

DESIGNERS: HUMBERTO & FERNANDO CAMPANA
MANUFACTURER: GRENDENE
DATE: 2005
MATERIAL: MELFLEX
DIMENSIONS: VARIABLE

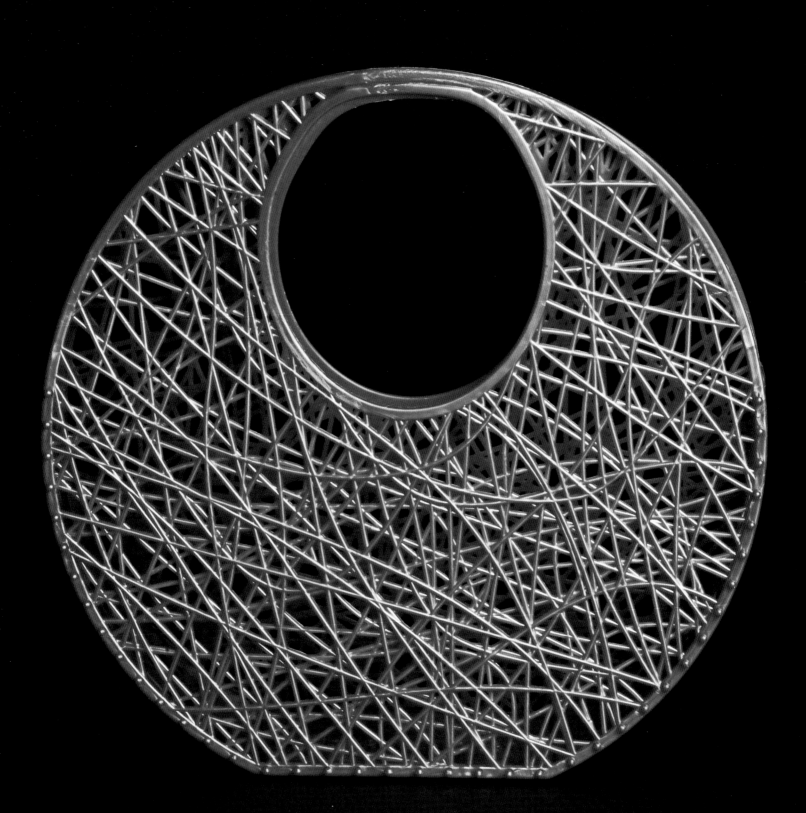

141

MERGING ART, DESIGN, AND CRAFT IS TYPICAL OF JONGERIUS'S WORK.
SHE JUXTAPOSES THE REFINEMENT OF MANUFACTURED PIECES WITH THE IMPERFECTIONS
OF THE HANDMADE, CREATING A NEW PARADIGM ALL HER OWN.

DESIGNER: HELLA JONGERIUS
MANUFACTURER: ARTECNICA
DATE: 2006
MATERIALS: CERAMIC, GLASS BEADS
DIMENSIONS: 5.5"H x 5.1"DIAM

Beads and Pieces

Hella Jongerius is known for mixing disciplines—blending industry and craft in her work. Beads and Pieces perfectly exemplifies this combination. She turned a functional object—a bowl—into an art object by piercing and beading through its surface, and adding a decorative beaded patch.

This curious bowl represents the cross-fertilization of different cultures and artistic disciplines. The manufacturer Artecnica paired Dutch designer Jongerius with Peru's Shipibo tribe through their program called Design with Conscience. The program brings together the talents of skilled designers and artisans in underdeveloped countries. With Beads and Pieces, Jongerius combined the traditional black pottery of Peru with the delicate beadwork of the Shipibo Indians. By hand-beading over the bowl's surface, she made it less functional and more decorative.

JAPANESE ARTIST YOSHITOMO NARA
TOOK ONE OF HIS PROVOCATIVE PAINTINGS
AND TURNED IT INTO AN EVEN MORE
PROVOCATIVE ASHTRAY.

Too Young To Die

Nara's artwork is part of a genre of Japanese pop art known as *kimo kawaii*, or "disgusting cute." His image of a toddler wearing a baby doll dress and a sinister expression while puffing on a cigarette, is simultaneously funny and macabre.

Adapting the painting for an everyday object introduced an element of interactivity. How is the user going to feel stubbing out a cigarette on this enigmatic character, or reading the words on the rim, jotted in a childlike hand?

Viewing Too Young To Die as a painting has a singular impact; but seeing those same images cleverly integrated into an ashtray makes the message that much more powerful. Nara successfully navigates the tricky boundary between art and design, and as a result reaches farther and hits his audiences harder.

DESIGNER: YOSHITOMO NARA
MANUFACTURER: CEREALART
DATE: 2002
MATERIAL: CERAMIC
DIMENSIONS: 1.25"H X 10"DIAM

Ball OO na stool

MORE THAN 500 PINK, ORANGE, YELLOW, RED, GREEN, AND PURPLE BALLOONS ARE WRAPPED, TWISTED, AND TIED BY HAND TO A SOLID WOOD STOOL TO MAKE BALLOONA.

It's obvious from looking at this piece that the designer loves bright colors. "I think color is just another tool to manipulate alongside finish, form, etc. I have an affinity for bright colors and was researching the use, reuse, and appreciation of everyday objects," explains Natalie Kruch.

Kruch tried and rejected raffia, leather, different types of fabric, and even elastic bands before hitting on balloons. The strength of their colors and the use of this festive material equally contribute to the chair's effect. But how do you create the perfect balance of color? What's the desired proportion of pink to red and yellow to purple? Here's where the talent of the designer/artist is revealed: what at first glance appears to be random is in fact a strategic mix of colors evoking a joyful response.

DESIGNER: NATALIE KRUCH
MANUFACTURER: UMBRA
DATE: 2010
MATERIALS: 500+ BALLOONS, WOODEN FRAME
DIMENSIONS: 17"H x 14"W x 14"D

The Honeycomb Vase

Collaborations are not uncommon in creative fields, but designer Tomáš Gabzdil Libertíny created a buzz in the design world when he chose an unusual partner. Using the hard work and skill of 40,000 honeybees, he developed a novel process to manipulate their honeycomb-building instincts.

He begins by constructing a framework made of thin sheets of beeswax that are imprinted with a honeycomb pattern. The bees take it from there—they follow the hexagonal pattern and slowly build honeycomb around the form. One week later, a delicate beeswax vase is revealed. For Libertíny, the iconic vase shape was obvious. A vase holds flowers—the flowers supply bees with nectar to make beeswax—and now bees use beeswax to build his vase.

BEE LABOR ISN'T CHEAP: THIS VASE COSTS $30,000!

DESIGNER: TOMÁŠ GABZDIL LIBERTÍNY
MANUFACTURER: STUDIO LIBERTÍNY
DATE: 2007
MATERIALS: BEESWAX
DIMENSIONS: 9.5"H X 6.25"DIAM

chapter 7

sustainability

DESIGNERS ARE PROBLEM SOLVERS. They tackle everything from annoying day-to-day problems to the major issues of our age. Look closely and you'll note that designs being produced in a specific time period are often shaped by the nature of that era's problems. Since the turn of the last century, sustainability—the ability to maintain an ecological balance on Earth—has been approaching crisis mode. Even as we consume the resources of our planet faster than they can be renewed, we're creating a surplus of waste. To ameliorate this mess, designers and manufacturers are increasingly employing "responsible design." Designers are always looking at sustainability from new angles and with the benefit of new research. They create products that are biodegradable and recyclable, and use less material for production and packaging. Other products reduce overall consumption by having longer life spans and easy-to-replace parts. Ultimately, sustainability-minded designers are busy developing creative ways to lessen our impact on the environment and to restore the ecological balance. Some have said that design can change the world. These designers know that first we have to save it.

152

Tide Chandelier

What comes to mind when you think of recycling? Probably not chandeliers. Stuart Haygarth's Tide chandelier shatters preconceptions about design and recycling: design from found objects must have an earthy aesthetic, and chandeliers are never ever made from trash. Haygarth created Tide with more than 1,000 pieces of rubbish he found washed up on the beach at Dungeness in southeast England. His mastery is in the transformation of these discarded plastic bottles, toothbrushes, and eyeglasses into a stunning sphere. His process is sorting, categorizing, and assembling—he hardly manipulates the objects themselves. The resulting shape is a nod to the moon, whose tidal pull delivers his raw materials. How poetic. From trash picker to lyrical designer, Haygarth has turned refuse into resplendence.

DESIGNER: STUART HAYGARTH
MANUFACTURER: STUART HAYGARTH
DATE: 2004
MATERIAL: MAN-MADE DEBRIS
DIMENSIONS: 59"DIAM

Moscardino Spork

154

With the growing awareness of limited natural resources, the impetus to design products using recyclable and biodegradable materials has grown from a trend into a movement. From product design to architecture, environmental responsibility has become an essential component of contemporary design.

Designers know that even the smallest products can have a big impact. The Moscardino spork replaces the plastic forks and spoons typically used for picnics and meals on the go. Those plastics derive from mineral oil, a nonrenewable resource, and can take centuries to decompose. IN CONTRAST, THE CORNSTARCH-BASED PLASTIC USED TO CREATE MOSCARDINO ACHIEVES 90% DEGRADATION IN ABOUT FIFTY DAYS UNDER NORMAL COMPOSTING CONDITIONS. Moscardino can also be hand-washed and reused repeatedly. Lastly, and most obviously, it cuts down on the number of utensils needed to picnic since the tool is two—a spoon and fork—in one responsible little package.

DESIGNERS: GIULIO IACCHETTI & MATTEO RAGNI
MANUFACTURER: PANDORA DESIGN
DATE: 2000
MATERIAL: 100% BIODEGRADABLE CORNSTARCH-BASED PLASTIC
DIMENSIONS: 3.5"L

THE PLASTIC CANOPY OF BRELLI BLOCKS RAIN AND UV RAYS.
IT BIODEGRADES COMPLETELY IN A COMPOST OR LANDFILL.
AND ON A WINDY DAY, EVEN IF YOU CAN'T STAND UP,
BRELLI CAN, IN WINDS OF UP TO 40 MILES PER HOUR.

Brelli

The ubiquitous, inexpensive black nylon umbrella sold on sidewalks takes more than a hundred years to biodegrade—and it lasts only a few rainstorms before ending up broken and abandoned on the street. The site of one such impromptu umbrella graveyard, on a rainy New York day, inspired fashion designer and product development professional Pam Zonsius to create an alternative that is both beautiful and environmentally responsible.

Zonsius already knew what Brelli's bamboo frame would resemble. Decades earlier she'd sat on a beach looking at the tiny tropical umbrella in her drink and wondered why no one had designed an umbrella using the structural webbing of a tiny Asian parasol.

Creating the canopy was more complex. She wanted to use a plastic that would be strong enough to withstand 40 mph winds and be biodegradable. Evaluating existing plastic products, Zonsius found they ran the risk of biodegrading when exposed to the elements, or they contained harsh chemicals. "There was nothing available on the market that would fit my requirements," Zonsius says. "So I had to invent it."

DESIGNER: PAM ZONSIUS
MANUFACTURER: PAM&CO
DATE: 2005
MATERIALS: BAMBOO, BIODEGRADABLE PVC, COTTON STRING
DIMENSIONS: 29"L x 45"DIAM

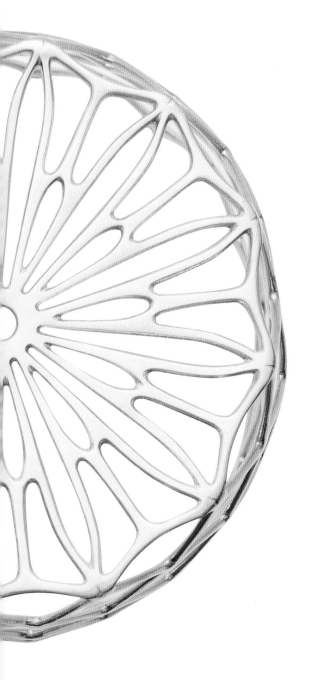

Kaktus

Enrico Bressan's Kaktus stool weighs a mere 4.4 pounds, but it can hold up to almost a thousand. It took Bressan three years to figure out how to create this powerful structure with such a minimal amount of material. This lightweight piece also has minimal impact on the Earth's resources. It's made from 100% recycled aluminum.

THE DESIGNER FOUND THE SOLUTION IN NATURE, specifically in the fibrous skeleton of the Staghorn Cholla cactus, which grows wild in the Sonoran desert. Bressan is one of a growing number of designers engaging in biomimicry, or the adoption of nature's time-tested structures and systems for human-centered designs.

Bressan's design process embodies an ideal relationship by borrowing his ideas from nature and by using recycled materials—like a good friend, he returned the favor by giving back.

DESIGNER: ENRICO BRESSAN
MANUFACTURER: ARTECNICA
DATE: 2010
MATERIAL: RECYCLED ALUMINUM
DIMENSIONS: 18"H x 17"DIAM

Stretch Bag

is a piece of billboard transformed by a simple die cut—a machine stamps out the pattern, which is designed to use minimal material with minimal waste. A single piece of material expands to create each bag, which can hold up to 33 pounds of cargo. No glue or stitching is required.

Artecnica, the manufacturer, has an exclusive partnership with TBWA, an ad agency network representing Apple, Adidas, Absolut Vodka, and other global clients. As a consumer, you're never sure which company's ad your bag embodied in its previous life. Each bag is different, depending on where it's cut from the billboard.

Advertising and industrial design have always had a strong connection—the former aids in creating desire for the latter. What better way for the ad industry to give back than by supplying the material for a recycled product.

DESIGNER: STUDIO ARTECNICA
MANUFACTURER: ARTECNICA
DATE: 2009
MATERIAL: RECYCLED BILLBOARD
DIMENSIONS: 28"H x 16"DIAM

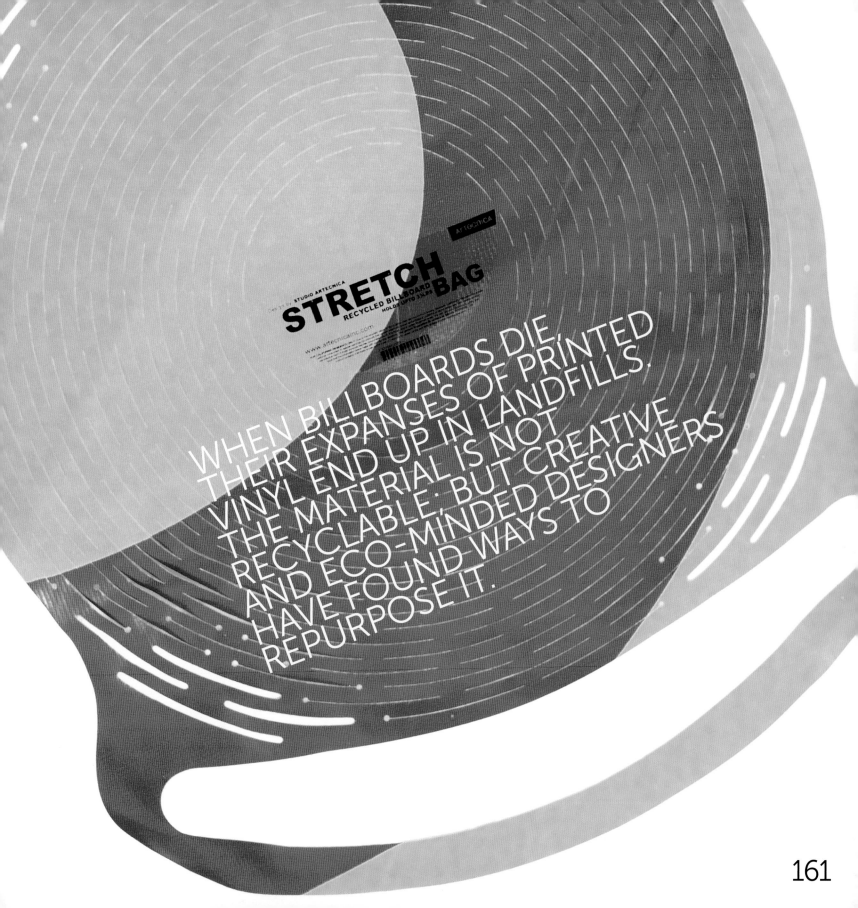

STRETCH BAG
Des 3n by STUDIO ARTECNICA
ARTECNICA
RECYCLED BILLBOARD HOLDS UPTO 3XLBS
www.artecnicainc.com

WHEN BILLBOARDS DIE THEIR EXPANSES OF PRINTED VINYL END UP IN LANDFILLS. THE MATERIAL IS NOT RECYCLABLE, BUT CREATIVE AND ECO-MINDED DESIGNERS HAVE FOUND WAYS TO REPURPOSE IT.

Plumen

PLUMEN IS THE WORLD'S FIRST DESIGNER LIGHTBULB.

Pre-Plumen, there were very few variations in the shape of a bulb. As Nicolas Roope of Hulger observed, "It's strange that the bulb, an object so synonymous with ideas, is almost entirely absent of imagination." Compact fluorescent bulbs use 80% less energy and last eight times longer than a traditional incandescent bulb. These advantages "negate the need for disposability (and invisibility)," and inspired Hulger to place the lightbulb in a new context.

In the tubular formation of these energy-efficient bulbs, the designers saw an opportunity for "drawing in the air" with light. Plumen was just one of many abstract, sculptural forms conceived during development. The chosen form looks different from every angle. Plumen doesn't need to be hidden behind a lampshade. The bulb itself is the lamp. At the same time its silhouette suggests the shape of an incandescent bulb, reminding us just how far the bulb has come, both in terms of sustainability and aesthetic design.

DESIGNER: SAMUEL WILKINSON/HULGER
MANUFACTURER: HULGER
DATE: 2011 (PROTOTYPE 2007)
MATERIALS: GLASS, ABS PLASTIC
DIMENSIONS: 7.5"H

164

Flip Flop Vase

Flip-flops may evoke images of the beach and carefree summers, but they are also the primary form of footwear for millions of people around the world. Cheap and disposable, they're worn until they fall apart. Once discarded the flip-flops often wind up in sewers, rivers, and eventually the sea. Every year more than 60,000 pounds of old flip-flops wash onto the beaches of eastern Africa. Dutch designer Diederik Schneemann, working in collaboration with a flip-flop recycling company in Kenya, turns this trash into treasure by employing the reclaimed rubber as raw material for a line of playful vases and lamps.

THE DIRTY FLIP-FLOPS WERE TRANSFORMED BY FIRST SANDING OFF LAYERS OF GRIME TO REVEAL THE ORIGINAL BRIGHT COLORS. SCHNEEMANN CUT THIS CLEANED RUBBER INTO SMALL SQUARES AND GLUED THE PIECES TOGETHER. HE THEN SCULPTED IT INTO ITS FINAL SHAPE. Most of the reclaimed flip-flops were either pink or blue, and it was this childlike color palette that inspired Schneemann to create his whimsical designs. Looking at this artful and dramatic vase, you would never have a clue that it started out as filthy old shoes.

DESIGNER: DIEDERIK SCHNEEMANN
MANUFACTURER: DIEDERIK SCHNEEMANN
DATE: 2011
MATERIALS: VARIOUS RUBBERS
DIMENSIONS: 19.7"H X 17.75"W X 15.75"D

DESIGNER: JAIME SALM AND ALEX UNDI
MANUFACTURER: MIO
DATE: 2012
MATERIAL: CARDBOARD
DIMENSIONS: 6"H x 24"W x 24"DIAM

THE MISSION OF MIO IS TO SPREAD
"GREEN DESIRE" BY CREATING IRRESISTIBLE PRODUCTS
THAT HAPPEN TO BE GOOD FOR THE EARTH.
BUT ALL OF THESE ECOLOGICAL CONCERNS
ARE INTENDED TO REMAIN IN THE BACKGROUND.
LITERALLY.

FoldScapes

Is there anything more banal and characterless than the flat ceiling tiles that hover over millions of offices around the world? The design firm MIO has altered that landscape with FoldScapes, their inventive three-dimensional ceiling tile system. Made of recycled cardboard, the tiles come flat and are folded on site. Many aspects of the ceiling-tiles' sustainability aren't immediately obvious. The use of a single element and just one material means there's an economy of means in production. They're boxed as a set of 24 flat tiles, which reduces the product's packaging, shipping costs, and space required for storage. They fit within the 2x2 or 2x4 grid of the standard drop-ceiling frame, and rest inside without screws or bolts. The effect is dramatic, a smart architectural detail that looks like a million bucks but costs just a few.

Wooden Radio

"Less wood, more work."

That's Indonesian designer Singgih Kartono's philosophy. Train and employ as many people as possible to make objects using as little wood as possible. This is his formula for sustaining the local population and the living landscape of Kandangan, his native village in Central Java. Kartono returned to Kandangan after attending college and observed that the agricultural sector, long the economic backbone of the village, was deteriorating. "Having lost their farms, many villagers were forced to find jobs in the city or to stay in the village with only the bare minimum for survival," he says, "or to find new sources of income around the village that usually ended up exploiting the forest and nature."

He started his environmentally conscious company Magno as a vehicle through which to replace farming with craftsmanship. Kartono trained local workers to make products using wood, a renewable, local resource. He then set up a nursery to plant a tree for every one that was cut down.

As if establishing a new economy for his village wasn't enough, Kartono wields the styling of Wooden Radio as a tool in his campaign against overconsumption. Its classic look is timeless, increasing the product's lifecycle, and the wood is left uncoated, requiring the user to oil it periodically. The designer believes this nurturing relationship will encourage the radio's owner to treat it as an heirloom and, he hopes, hold onto it as one.

DESIGNER: SINGGIH S. KARTONO
MANUFACTURER: PIRANTI WORKS
DATE: 2006
MATERIALS: PINE, MAHOGANY, FABRIC
DIMENSIONS: 7.5"H x 7.5"W x 4.25"D

WASARA is compostable tableware that is elegant and sculptural. Like the finest porcelain it seems delicate but is very strong. Unlike porcelain it is intentionally ephemeral: the plates, bowls and cups are crafted from a thin composite of bamboo, reed pulp, and bagasse, a sugarcane byproduct. (No trees were harmed...)

Designer Shinichiro Ogata infused each piece with the Zen principles of aesthetics, including simplicity, unconventionality, and the element of surprise. Hidden delights unfold with use. Cup handles double as spouts. Plates have grooves to accommodate the hand. The bamboo utensils are notched and slide onto the tableware. Wasara really has only one flaw: it is too lovely to use just once. No one wants to throw it out.

DESIGNER: SHINICHIRO OGATA
MANUFACTURER: WASARA
DATE: 2008
MATERIAL: SUGAR CANE FIBER, BAMBOO, AND REED PULP
DIMENSIONS: VARIOUS

WASARA

Prolific designer Karim Rashid creates products across all categories. Each reflects his highly stylized aesthetic—sensual curves and bright colors—and his ambitious goal to use design to save the world.

DESIGN IS ABOUT REVISITING AND EVOLVING OUR CULTURE AND PHYSICAL LANDSCAPE…IT IS NOT ABOUT TRENDS…IT IS NOT ABOUT JUST FORM OR JUST FUNCTION; IT IS ABOUT PROGRESS AND EVOLVING OUR EXPERIENTIAL AESTHETIC WORLD. Karim Rashid

Bobble

That sounds like hyperbole, but Bobble, the first water bottle with a built-in potable filter, may have started a trend that will actually save the world. The carbon filter attached to the bottle's cap purifies tap water as you drink it. One of these filters equals 300 water bottles that you won't have to buy, and 300 water bottles that won't end up in a landfill. Bobble's bottle, cap, and filter are all recyclable.

Rashid came up against several specific challenges while developing Bobble. Achieving the correct contours for an ergonomic grip was important. He had to play around with the wall thickness before finding the minimum amount of plastic that would be strong enough to endure 300 fills. Finally, the bottle had to be flexible enough to spring back into its original shape after squeezing. As it turns out, this is an object that's not only environmentally friendly—it's environmentally necessary.

DESIGNER: KARIM RASHID
MANUFACTURER: MOVE COLLECTIVE
DATE: 2010
MATERIAL: PET
DIMENSIONS: 8.25"H x 2.75"DIAM

designforgood

The objects in this chapter illustrate the notion that design can dramatically improve the quality of everyone's life. More and more high-profile designers are applying their acute powers of critical thinking and problem solving to tools geared toward health, safety, and education. They are asking holistic, meaningful questions about objects as basic as pill bottles and fire extinguishers that were typically created by engineers or in-house staff. Some of these tools have not been redesigned in decades and need to be reassessed to meet the needs of the modern user. Other objects are being redesigned to fit into the lives of people from different cultures, in different countries, and at different socioeconomic levels. As designers continue to address the needs of those who may not have benefited from their focus in the past, everyone benefits.

New York City Condom Dispenser and Wrapper

Soon after launching its 2007 initiative to dispense free condoms citywide, the New York City Department of Health ran into a wall. Stores, bars, and other privately owned businesses weren't interested in displaying fishbowls full of condoms. Stakes were high—condoms are the most effective barrier to the transmission of HIV and unwanted pregnancies. In 2008, the city called on Yves Béhar to rebrand and redesign the condom dispenser and wrapper for a more "ownable look."

Béhar sought to reduce the stigma attached to condoms by making the forms inviting and familiar. The wrappers' design alludes to the New York City subway, whose graphics include large white numbers and letters in colored circles. By referencing that familiar iconography, Behar's design sends the message that condoms are commonplace—just like the subway, they're a part of everyday life.

The design of the dispenser is also referential: its dimpled shape emulates the imprint a condom leaves on the surface of a leather wallet. The dispensing method—the user reaches into the hole at the dispenser's base—is suggestive and fun. With the new campaign the number of condoms distributed bounced from 9 million to 39 million per year. Béhar's good design amplified the popularity of the NYC-branded condoms and, presumably, the popularity of safe sex.

DESIGNER: YVES BÉHAR/FUSEPROJECT
CLIENT: CITY OF NEW YORK
DATE: 2008
MATERIAL: PLASTIC
DIMENSIONS: 5.5"D x 18"DIAM

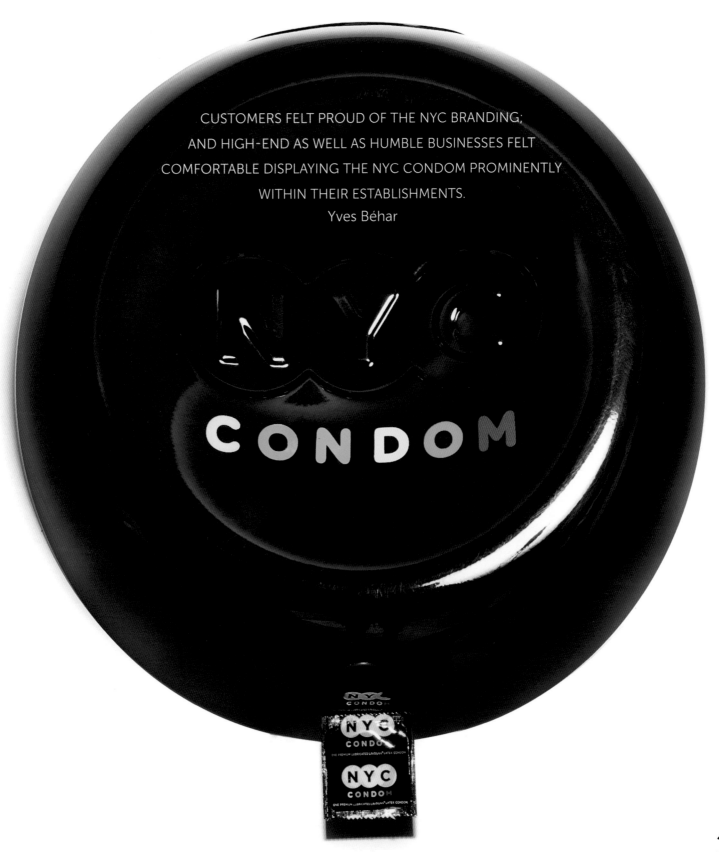

CUSTOMERS FELT PROUD OF THE NYC BRANDING;
AND HIGH-END AS WELL AS HUMBLE BUSINESSES FELT
COMFORTABLE DISPLAYING THE NYC CONDOM PROMINENTLY
WITHIN THEIR ESTABLISHMENTS.
Yves Béhar

CONDOM

XO Laptop
One Laptop per Child

Nicholas Negroponte founded the One Laptop per Child (OLPC) project in 2005 with the ambitious goal of getting laptop computers into the hands of millions of children in developing countries. He knew that access to technology is essential for competing in the industrialized world.

Yves Béhar and his firm fuseproject were the ideal collaborators. Béhar's core philosophy is design as an agent of change. "We need to initiate an emphasis on the notion of 'Design for Good,'" he has said. "We have a responsibility to the world around us."

Designing a computer for children from Argentina to Africa who had no prior exposure to technology was a significant challenge. The laptop had to be low-cost (the goal was $100) and integrate highly advanced technology with a thoughtful design that considered the specific users and their varied conditions.

These concerns are reflected in the XO laptop, whose sturdy plastic clamshell is drop-proof and spill-proof. The plastic bumper encircling XO protects it from dust and water and acts as a palm rest when the computer is open. The laptop's screen displays in full-color and in high-contrast black and white to be readable in pitch dark or bright sun. To appeal to his young clients, Béhar made sure to infuse XO's branding and features with whimsy and expressiveness. The WiFi antennas, or "rabbit ears," lend the computer personality. And the potential to personalize the case's XO logo—there are 400 possible color combinations—is important if every kid in town is going to have the same computer.

THE OLPC PROGRAM ULTIMATELY ISN'T ABOUT DISTRIBUTING COMPUTERS— IT'S ABOUT DISSEMINATING EDUCATION, THE ONE TRUE WEAPON IN THE FIGHT AGAINST POVERTY, IGNORANCE, AND EVEN DISEASE.

DESIGNER: YVES BÉHAR/FUSEPROJECT
MANUFACTURER: QUANTA COMPUTER & OLPC
DATE: 2007
MATERIALS: ABS, RUBBER
DIMENSIONS: 1.5"H x 9"W x 9.5"D

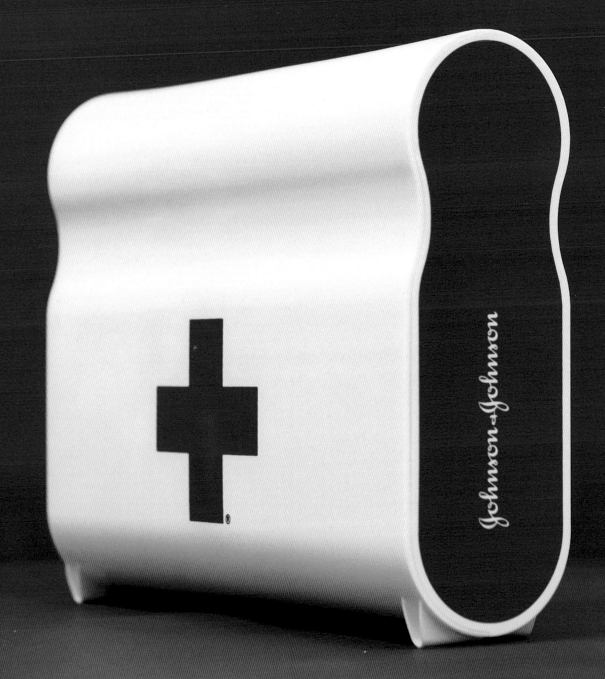

THIS DESIGN IS A PERFECT MARRIAGE OF FORM AND FUNCTION. IN A NEW AND EXCITING WAY,
THE DESIGN OF THIS OBJECT INFORMS THE USER WHAT IT DOES, HOW IT IS USED, AND WHAT IT
STANDS FOR…WE GAVE IT BACK AN IDENTITY, AND A PRETTY MODERN ONE AT THAT.

Harry Allen

Johnson & Johnson First Aid Kit

When Johnson & Johnson asked Harry Allen to redesign its First Aid Kit, he knew he was being asked to create a new classic. "The First Aid Kit is an icon in and of itself," he says, "so to give it a new form is a delicate matter." Over the years, the healthcare behemoth's handsome metal kits had evolved into disposable plastic cases. Rather than continuing to fill landfills, the company wanted to introduce a "dynamic new form" with a longer lifecycle—something people would want to hold on to and refill when supplies ran low. The resulting design has a slender, vertical profile that makes the box easier to store and take off the shelf. (No more piling toiletries atop a kit buried at the bottom of the cabinet.) The figure-eight shape manages to integrate a handle that "conveys a sense of grab-and-go urgency."

DESIGNER: HARRY ALLEN
MANUFACTURER: JOHNSON & JOHNSON
DATE: 2008
MATERIAL: POLYPROPYLENE
DIMENSIONS: 8"H x 10"W x 2.75"D

181

Deborah Adler redesigned the standard pill bottle for her design school thesis after her grandmother accidently took her grandfather's pills. It was an easy mistake. The only differences on the bottles' labels were the dosage and the patients' first names (Helen versus Herman). Thankfully, Helen was okay, but Adler decided the potential consequences of this mistake were far too dangerous to ignore.

When Target saw Adler's work, the company joined forces with her to create the ClearRx bottles for their pharmacies. The new bottles have a wedge shape that's easy to grip and provides a large flat surface for text. This is a significant improvement over hard-to-read round bottles covered with labels and warning stickers.

With ClearRx, all the information is arranged according to a hierarchy that reflects a patient's needs. Vital data (patient name, drug name, how to take the medication) appear on the front, and warnings are listed on the back. Adler worked with legendary graphic designer Milton Glaser to make the warning-label icons more intuitive. A small text-magnifier and a folded information pamphlet are tucked neatly behind the back label. One of the most practical changes with the new bottle is a colored rubber ring around the top. There are six different colors to choose from, allowing each family member to have his or her own. Certainly, if Grandma Helen had had the benefit of these smartly designed bottles, she would never have grabbed the wrong pills.

Target Clear
RX Pharmacy Bottles

DESIGNER: DEBORAH ADLER
MANUFACTURER: SETCO
DATE: 2004
MATERIAL: PET
DIMENSIONS: 4"H x 2.25"W x 1.5"D

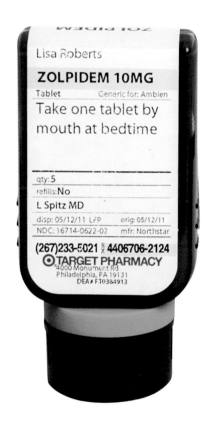

Lisa Roberts

ZOLPIDEM 10MG

Tablet   Generic for: Ambien

Take one tablet by
mouth at bedtime

qty: 5
refills: No

L Spitz MD

disp: 05/12/11 LFP   orig: 05/12/11
NDC: 16714-0622-02   mfr: Northstar

(267)233-5021 ‖ 4406706-2124
⊙ TARGET PHARMACY
4000 Monument Rd
Philadelphia, PA 19131
DEA# FT0384913

Height-Adjustable
Tub Rail

This bathtub rail by Michael Graves is revelatory because its form and aesthetics do not look or feel medicinal. The tall silhouette is architectural—even beautiful—and the distinctive colors, soft curves, and chubby lines are warm and appealing. There are playful elements, too, like the oversized orange knob and the soap holder's contoured pattern, resembling waves. The orange accents work double-duty by signifying action.

Historically, tub rails and other products designed for older and disabled people have been unattractive and poorly functional—an unforgivable oversight when the population in question so greatly needs design that works and doesn't stigmatize. Architect Michael Graves discovered this firsthand in 2003 when a spinal infection paralyzed him from the chest down. As he recounted to Metropolis magazine, the sink in his hospital room was too far for him to reach. The mirror was too high for him to see himself shaving.

Graves believes design shouldn't stop when people slow down or get older. It should continue to improve the quality of a person's life throughout the course of a life. And he continues to humanize object after object in the broad range of health and medical equipment most of us will encounter at some point in our lives, all the while inspiring other designers to follow suit. Deep into an impressive career Graves suffered a personal misfortune, and he responded to paralysis with the most able-minded and impactful action.

DESIGNER: MICHAEL GRAVES DESIGN GROUP
MANUFACTURER: DRIVE MEDICAL DESIGN AND MANUFACTURING
DATE: 2006
MATERIALS: ENAMELED STEEL, ABS, NYLON
DIMENSIONS: 20.75"H X 17.875"W X 9.25"D

Etón FRX3 Emergency Radio

HURRICANE? FLOOD? EARTHQUAKE? FLAT TIRE?

The Etón FRX3 has you covered. The compact device integrates nearly every gadget needed in an emergency, including a digital radio (with seven NOAA weather stations), LED flashlight, red flashing beacon light, built-in cell phone charger, radio antenna, and four sources of power (battery, electrical plug, hand crank, and solar panel). These extensive features are packaged in a streamlined tool that is simply designed and intuitive to use.

One minute of cranking or sitting in the sun gets you fifteen minutes of radio or flashlight time. You may as well practice because someday, whether your power goes out or you find yourself roadside without a spare tire, you might need it.

DESIGNER: DAN HARDEN/WHIPSAW
MANUFACTURER: ETÓN CORPORATION
DATE: 2012
MATERIALS: PLASTIC, METAL, LED LIGHTS, SOLAR PANEL
DIMENSIONS: 7.875"H X 7"W X 3.5"D

Peter Arnell tackled the ubiquitous red fire extinguisher—an ugly yet indispensable household object—to provide an alternative that's both appealing and easy to use, even when the user is in panic mode. Designed in the 1950s, the traditional red extinguisher despite its flaws—functionally awkward, aesthetically displeasing and intimidating—has remained virtually unchanged for more than half a century.

"IN MY EARLY INVESTIGATION I STUDIED HOW STEVE JOBS APPROACHED THE IPOD. IF YOU LOOK CAREFULLY YOU REALIZE THAT IT WAS A MASTERFUL JOB OF DESIGNING AND PACKAGING AN EXTERIOR TO HOUSE EXISTING TECHNOLOGIES."

Peter Arnell

Home Hero

Home Hero's sleek silhouette and contemporary palette blend into the interiors of most kitchens, so it's more likely to be at arm's reach in an emergency. Its most essential features are also its most prominent: the safety pin and the trigger on the extinguisher's handle. The simple three-step directions, positioned on the extinguisher to face the user, are impossible to miss.

Arnell made Home Hero's deployment mechanism balanced and ergonomic—"more like a pistol for more precise squirting," he says. The extinguisher can be operated with one hand, leaving the other hand free to dial 911. Now there's no excuse not to be a home hero.

DESIGNER: ARNELL GROUP
MANUFACTURER: KIDDE
DATE: 2007
MATERIALS: VARIOUS
DIMENSIONS: 16"H x 3.5"DIAM

See Better
to Learn Better

Each year, half a million schoolchildren in Mexico need glasses but go without because their families can't afford them. As a tool for learning, corrective lenses rank up there with pencils and books. Any educator will confirm that to see better is to learn better.

To correct this imbalance, designer Yves Béhar partnered with the government of Mexico, lens manufacturer Augen Optics, and the non-profit organization Ver Bien to make and donate eyeglasses. As with One Laptop per Child, Béhar's clients ranged in age from 6 to 18. His challenge was to change their perception of spectacles from a visible handicap to something fun and fashionable. Durability was another top priority.

BÉHAR'S SOLUTION WAS TO USE A PLASTIC THAT'S VIRTUALLY INDESTRUCTIBLE AND TO OFFER A CHOICE OF FIVE FRAME STYLES, EACH MADE OF TWO PIECES THAT SNAP TOGETHER. WITH SEVEN COLOR OPTIONS FOR MIXING AND MATCHING, THERE ARE MORE THAN 25,000 OPPORTUNITIES FOR EACH STUDENT TO EXPRESS HIS OR HER PERSONAL STYLE. A RANGE OF THREE FRAME SIZES AND INTERCHANGEABLE NOSE PADS ENSURE A BEST FIT FOR EVERYONE.

The snap-together frames encourage customization, but also make assembly more cost-effective. Instead of using the traditional, more expensive heating process for shaping the frames, the manufacturer pops in the lenses, welds the nose bridge, and fastens the glasses with hinge screws. When necessary, the old lenses are easily swapped out for a new prescription.

Béhar's vision is honed and ambitious. He foresees a network of See Better to Learn Better initiatives around the globe, using Mexico's program as a model.

DESIGNER: YVES BÉHAR/FUSEPROJECT
MANUFACTURER: AUGEN OPTICS
DATE: 2010
MATERIAL: GRILAMID (OR POLYAMIDE 12)
DIMENSIONS: VARIABLE

KOZMOS BLOCKS, KARIM RASHID

resources

bios A–Z

Deborah Adler (American, born 1975) received her MFA in design from New York's School of Visual Arts (SVA) in 2002. For her thesis project, she designed a comprehensive system for packaging prescription medicine. She brought this innovation to Target, and together they developed the ClearRx system. Adler established her firm, Deborah Adler Design, in 2008. Much of her work is in the medical industry, for clients such as Johnson & Johnson and Medline, for whom she designs products, packaging, labeling, identity, and information systems. Her designs are in the permanent collection of the Museum of Modern Art in New York, have been shown at the Cooper-Hewitt, National Design Museum as part of the National Design Triennial, and were featured in a solo exhibition titled *From Master's Thesis to Medicine Cabinet* at SVA, New York, in 2006. deborahadlerdesign.com

Harry Allen (American, born 1964) received a master's degree in industrial design from New York's Pratt Institute in 1992. After working for Prescriptives Cosmetics designing point-of-purchase displays, he opened his own studio in 1993. That same year Allen's first line of furniture, Living Systems, was presented at the International Contemporary Furniture Fair in New York. He attracted the attention of Murray Moss, who hired him to design the iconic Moss Gallery in New York. Since then, Allen has expanded from designing furniture and interiors to products, lighting, graphics, and exhibitions, His Reality Series for Areaware, launched in 2004, has garnered international attention, and Allen's work can be found in the permanent collections of the Museum of Modern Art in New York, the Brooklyn Museum of Art, and the Philadelphia Museum of Art. harryallendesign.com

Ron Arad (Israeli, born 1951) attended the Bezalel Academy of Art in Jerusalem (1971–73) and the Architectural Association School of Architecture in London (1974–79). In 1981, he opened One Off, a gallery-studio for experimental design, which was later renamed Ron Arad Associates. His early work focused on singular pieces of sculptural furniture, often made out of welded steel. Arad's iconic Big Easy chair, originally constructed from sheets of tempered steel, resembled a cartoonish, overstuffed upholstered armchair. It was later remade out of polyurethane and put into production by the Italian manufacturer Moroso. In addition to his "one-off," individual pieces, he has designed for Alessi, Cassina, Driade, Kartell, and Magis. Arad has also continuously pursued architectural projects, including the cutting-edge Maserati showroom headquarters (2003) in Modena, Italy, and the highly acclaimed Design Museum Holon (2009), Israel's first national museum dedicated to design and architecture. Recent large-scale exhibitions of his work have been held at the Centre Georges Pompidou in Paris (2008), the Museum of Modern Art in New York (2009), and the Stedelijk Museum Amsterdam (2012). ronarad.com.uk

BANANA BOWL, HARRY ALLEN

194

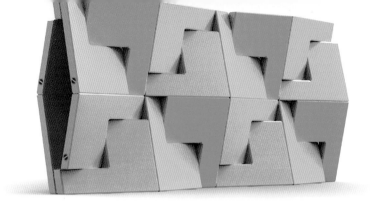

QUADROR, DROR BENSHETRIT

Arnell Group is a branding, marketing, communications, and design firm founded by Peter Arnell in 1979. The New York–based company specializes in product and brand innovation, developing projects from initial concept to market introduction. Its client list includes Belvedere Vodka, Donna Karan/DKNY, Fila, Jose Cuervo International, Masterfoods/M&M's, PepsiCo, Samsung, and Reebok/RBK. In 2006 the agency teamed up with The Home Depot to launch ORANGE WORKS, a partnership aimed at "creating innovative products that will embody high levels of functionality, next-generation technology, consumer appeal, style and design." The Home Hero fire extinguisher was a result of this partnership, and it won the 2007 Industrial Designers Society of America IDEA Gold Award in the consumer products category. arnell.com

Maarten Baas (Dutch, born Germany, 1978) graduated from the Design Academy Eindhoven in 2002. His thesis project was a collection of burnt furniture titled *Smoke*, and its success led to a solo exhibition at Moss Gallery in New York. For the exhibit, he burned design classics by Gaudí, Eames, Rietveld, and Sottsass. In 2005 Baas established a studio with Bas den Herder, who is responsible for production. The studio's groundbreaking projects combine the irregularities of handmade processes with precision engineering. Just how far should the furniture burn so it can retain its structural integrity when coated with resin? How much clay should be padded around a steel structure to give it a sense of fragility? His work has been exhibited at the Victoria & Albert Museum in London, the Stedelijk Museum Amsterdam, the Design Museum in London, and the Groninger Museum in the Netherlands. In 2009 Baas was awarded Designer of the Year at Design Miami. maartenbaas.com

Yves Béhar (Swiss, born 1967) studied design in Europe and has a degree in industrial design from the Art Center College of Design in Pasadena, California. In 1999 he founded Fuseproject, an industrial design and branding firm with offices in San Francisco and New York. Fuseproject clients include for-profit and non-profit organizations. Béhar's core philosophy is that "sustainability and notions of social good are the new values of the twenty-first century, and designers need to integrate them into every project they do."[1] His designs have garnered more than 150 awards, and his work is in the permanent collections of museums including the Centre Georges Pompidou in Paris; the Museum of Modern Art in New York; the Neue Sammlung, State Museum of Applied Arts in Munich; and the Chicago Art Institute. fuseproject.com

SAYL CHAIR, YVES BÉHAR

Dror Benshetrit (Israeli, born 1977) studied at the Design Academy Eindhoven and founded Studio Dror in New York in 2002. His focus is on innovation in design, technology, and the unusual use of materials. An element of variable movement is often integrated into his projects, whether an expandable hard-case travel bag for Tumi or a modular shelving system for Target. In 2006 Benshetrit developed a new structural support system made up of interlocking L-shaped pieces. Titled QuaDror, it can be configured into everything from furniture to bridges to buildings. Dror's awards include the iF Product Design Award (2006) and the Good Design Award from the Japan Institute of Design Promotion (2008 and 2010). His work can be found in the permanent collections of the Metropolitan Museum of Art and the Museum of Arts and Design in New York, the Eretz Israel Museum in Tel Aviv, and the Staatliches Museum in Munich. studiodror.com

Tord Boontje (Dutch, born 1968) studied industrial design at the Design Academy in Eindhoven and received a master's degree from the Royal College of Art in London in 1994. He founded Studio Tord Boontje in London 1996, and in 2009 he was named Professor and Head of Design Products at the Royal College of Art. His distinctive style takes inspiration from nature, and unlike many contemporary designers, he believes "that modernism does not mean minimalism, that contemporary does not forsake tradition, and that technology does not abandon people and senses." He has won multiple awards and is in the permanent collections of the Museum of Modern Art and the Cooper-Hewitt, National Design Museum in New York; the Victoria & Albert Museum in London; the San Francisco Museum of Modern Art; and the Stedeljik Museum Amsterdam, among others. tordboontje.com

Bould Design is a product development studio founded by Fred Bould, a graduate of Carnegie-Mellon and Stanford Universities. The Silicon Valley–based firm is "dedicated to exploring new forms, functions, materials and meanings for products." Their clients include Nest Labs, Logitech, Nambe, and Pablo, and the work they produce is highly diverse. The studio has been granted many awards including the 2012 Red Dot Design Award, several CES (Consumer Electronics Show) Design and Innovation Awards, the ID Magazine Design Review, and the GOOD Design Award. Their work is in the SFMoMA Permanent Design Collection in San Francisco. bould.com

Ronan Bouroullec (French, born 1971) & Erwan Bouroullec (French, born 1976) studied at École Nationale Supérieure des Arts Décoratifs in Paris and at École Nationale Supérieure de Cergy-Pontoise, respectively. After graduating, Ronan began working as a designer, and in 1997, he presented Disintegrated Kitchen at the Salon du Meuble in Paris. This customizable and portable kitchen unit caught the attention of the architect and designer Giulio Cappellini. When Erwan graduated in 1999, he joined his brother to work on several commissions for Cappellini, including the tree-house-like loft bed Lit Clos and the Hole furniture series. The brothers quickly developed a signature style described by Erwan as "deliberately very simple with an element of humour."[2] "Usually our work is strongest when we disagree, because that's when we push each other to go further," says Ronan.[3] Their designs have won numerous awards, including "Best of the Best" Red Dot Design Awards (2005, 2008), the Compasso d'Oro (2011), and 2011 Designer of the Year Award at Now! Maison & Objet. Work by the Bouroullecs is in the permanent collections of Musée National d'Art Moderne, Centre Georges Pompidou and Musée des Arts Décoratifs in Paris, the Museum of Modern Art in New York, the Art Institute of Chicago, and the Design Museum in London. bouroullec.com

John Brauer (Danish, born 1960) graduated from the KEA Copenhagen School of Design and Technology with a degree in architecture and has an MBA in innovation from the Danish Technological University. He founded the design company Essey around the philosophy that form should represent the nature of an object—a trashcan should look like crumpled paper, a fly swatter should look like a fly. Among his awards are the Good Design Award (2005, Japan) the Red Dot Design Award (2007), and the iF Product Design Award (2007). essey.com

Enrico Bressan (Italian, born 1960) studied engineering at Florida Atlantic University and California State University, Northridge, where he received a master's degree in 1986. That same year he and Tahmineh Javanbakht cofounded Artecnica, a design studio focusing on architectural and interior design services for clients including Gianni Versace and Sebastian International. In 1993 Artecnica launched its first commercial product design line, designed by Bresssan and contributing designers. In 2001, it released the first Design with Conscience collection, for which world-famous designers partner with crafts communities in developing countries. Artecnica's award-winning products are in the permanent collections of the Museum of Modern Art in New York, the Victoria & Albert Museum in London, the Corning Museum of Glass, the Art Institute of Chicago, and the Stedelijk Museum in Amsterdam. artecnica.com

François Brument (French, born 1978) graduated from the École Nationale Supérieure de Création Industrielle in Paris. His work focuses on the exploration of digital design and production: "My aim is to investigate how thinking, conceiving, fabricating, distributing digitally can profoundly change the design practice."[4] While many designers use digital technologies as a tool, Brument has made technology part of the work itself. As a skilled computer programmer, he has invented systems that change the way an object is designed. To create a unique shade for his KiLight, users interact with the program by moving their bodies, thus changing the shape of the lampshade. This can be done infinitely, creating a series of shades with no two alike. Brument's work was included in the 2008 exhibition *Design and the Elastic Mind* at the Museum of Modern Art in New York, and is in the permanent collections of France's Fonds National d'Art Contemporain and the Centre Canadien d'Architecture in Montreal. in-flexions.com

Stephen Burks (American, born 1969) studied architecture at the Illinois Institute of Technology and product design at IIT's Institute of Design in Chicago as well as attending Columbia University's Graduate School of Architecture. In 1997 he opened his New York studio, Readymade Projects. Burks's work bridges the sophisticated designs of the industrial world with the handmade crafts of developing nations. His projects include retail interiors, packaging, consumer products, lighting, furniture, and home accessories. Among his accolades are the IIT Alumni Professional Achievement Award, the Brooklyn Museum/Modernism Young Designer Award (2008), and a United States Artists, Architecture & Design Target Fellowship Grant for his outstanding work in product design (2008). In 2011 Burks held his first solo exhibition, *Man-Made*, at the Studio Museum in Harlem, where he collaborated with artisans from Africa, Peru, and India. readymadeprojects.com

Humberto Campana (Brazilian, born 1953) & Fernando Campana (Brazilian, born 1961) founded Estudio Campana in São Paulo in 1983. Humberto is a self-taught artist with a degree in law, and Fernando has a degree in architecture. They are inspired by the streets of Brazil and often combine low-tech materials such as cardboard, rope, fabric, wood scraps, bamboo, and aluminum wire with high-end craftsmanship. The Campanas' breakout design, the Vermelha chair manufactured by Edra in 2007, is their best seller. Their limited edition Sushi chairs are highly collectible and have broken auction records. In 2008 they received the Designer of the Year Award at Design Miami. Works by the Campanas have been represented in galleries and are in the permanent collections of museums throughout the world including the Design Museum in London; the Centre Georges Pompidou in Paris; the Museum of Modern Art and the Cooper-Hewitt, National Design Museum in New York; and the Philadelphia Museum of Art. campanas.com

Julien Carretero (French, born 1983) studied industrial design in Paris and England. He went on to pursue a master's degree at the Design Academy Eindhoven, under the direction of Gijs Bakker, while also working in the studio of Maarten Baas. Carretero's main interest deals with considering the production of objects as a growing process—alive and unpredictable. By often creating his own manufacturing techniques, he aims at blurring the border between serial and handmade production. juliencarretero.com

Gabriele Chiave (French, born 1978) studied industrial design at the Istituto Europeo di Design in Milan. From 2002 to 2006 he assisted in the organization and development of workshops, nicknamed LPWK, organized by Laura Polinoro and Alessi, which allowed designers to collaborate on the development of new typologies and "meta-projects" for the company. Chiave's Tripod Trivet is the result of one of these workshops. He now lives and works in Amsterdam. gabrielechiave.com

James Dyson (British, born 1947) studied art and design in London at the Byam Shaw School of Art and the Royal College of Art. He is best known for inventing the first bagless vacuum cleaner, which took fifteen years and over 5,000 prototypes to perfect. When Dyson could not find a manufacturer for his patented Dual Cyclone™ vacuum technology, he established his own factory and research center in Wiltshire, England. He believes that function dictates form: "Everything on the Dyson Vacuum cleaner has a purpose. Its distinctive look is determined by the functionality, first and foremost. The clear bin isn't an artistic statement. It just shows you when you need to empty it."[5] In 2000, he received an honorary doctorate in engineering from the University of Bath and in 2006 was knighted by Queen Elizabeth II. dyson.com

Boje Estermann (Danish, born 1961) was CEO of a French company before he made a career change and enrolled in design school at the École Nationale Supérieure Création Industrielle in Paris, graduating in 1999. The following year he opened his own studio in Paris. Estermann's work is a combination of functionality, inspired by his Scandinavian roots, and emotion, reflecting his current life as a Parisian. "I would love to create a home where all functional things only appear when needed. The rest should be calm and pleasure."[6] His work is in the permanent collections of the Museum of Modern Art in New York, the Philadelphia Museum of Art, and the Musée d'Art Moderne in Saint Étienne Métropole.

Naoto Fukasawa (Japanese, born 1956) graduated with a degree in product design from Tokyo's Tama Art University in 1980. He worked for IDEO in San Francisco and became head of its Tokyo office. In 2003 he established Naoto Fukasawa Design and launched his own

DC07 VACUUM CLEANER, JAMES DYSON

SUSHI III CHAIR, HUMBERTO & FERNANDO CAMPANA

197

MICHAEL GRAVES FOR TARGET

brand of household products called ±0 (PlusMinusZero). His minimalist style stems from a philosophy he calls "Without Thought." As he explains, "People shouldn't really have to think about an object when they are using it. Not having to think about it makes the relationship between a person and an object run more smoothly. Finding ideas in people's spontaneous behavior and realizing these ideas in design is what Without Thought is about."[7] Fukasawa has won over fifty awards, including the American IDEA Gold Award. naotofukasawa.com

Stefan Geisbauer (German, born 1978) originally studied advertising photography in Munich and remained in the industry until 2009. His career as a product designer began with the Looksoflat lamp, a 2010 collaboration with the studio of Ingo Maurer. The lamp was chosen for the permanent collections of the Designmuseo in Helsinki and the Design Museum in London. Geisbauer is interested in the progress of design and acknowledging its history: "While in past centuries the inventions were in decoration and form, our times, beginning with the industrial revolution, are defined by . . . advances . . . in technology. It is important to remember that today's classics were yesterday's new thoughts. They do not spring forward from nothing, but are rooted in what has come before, either as revolution or evolution."[8]

Adam Goodrum (Australian, born 1972) studied industrial design at the University of Technology in Sydney. In 2004 he received the Bombay Sapphire Design Discovery Award and was selected as one of the most influential Australians in *Bulletin* magazine's "Smart 100" in the Design and Architecture category. In 2008 Goodrum's Stitch chair for Cappellini was selected as one of the year's best designs by the Design Museum in London. adamgoodrum.com

Michael Graves (American, born 1934) received his architectural training at the University of Cincinnati and Harvard University. He started his practice in 1964 in Princeton, New Jersey, and his early work was in the modernist style of architecture. By the 1970s, he gravitated to the postmodernist style using exaggerated classical elements (e.g., columns and loggias) and decorative facades. His populist work attracted the attention of the Italian manufacturer Alessi. Graves was one of the first architects to become a household name when he designed his well-known bird-whistle teakettle, Alessi's best-selling product of all time. He became even better known when he collaborated with Target to design a large collection of household products. Graves is a professor emeritus at Princeton University and has received thirteen honorary doctorates. michaelgraves.com

Konstantin Grcic (German, born 1961) was trained as a cabinetmaker before studying design at the Royal College of Art in London. He set up his own practice, Konstantin Grcic Industrial Design (KGID), in Munich in 1991, and has developed furniture, products, and lighting for some of the leading companies in the design field. He received the Compasso d'Oro for his Mayday lamp (2001) and for the MYTO chair (2011). Grcic's work is in the permanent collections of the Museum of Modern Art in New York and the Centre Georges Pompidou in Paris. In 2010, he received the Designer of the Year Award at Design Miami. konstantin-grcic.com

CHAIR_ONE, KONSTANTIN GRCIC

Zaha Hadid (Iraqi, born 1950) received a degree in mathematics from the American University of Beirut before studying at the Architectural Association School of Architecture in London. In 1980 she opened her own London-based practice, but it was not until 1994 that her first project was built, the Vitra Fire Station in Weil am Rhein, Germany. The fluidity and abstract elements of her architectural designs have in many cases required advancements in technology so that the projects could finally be realized. Hadid has created over 950 projects in forty-four countries and in 2004 was the first woman to be awarded the Pritzker Architecture Prize. In 2012, Zaha Hadid was awarded a DBE (Dame Commander of the Order of the British Empire). zaha-hadid.com

Dan Harden (American, born 1959) graduated from the College of Design, Architecture, and Art at the University of Cincinnati in 1982 with a degree in industrial design. Early in his career, he worked for several renowned design firms, including George Nelson Associates and Henry Dreyfuss Associates. In 1989 he became president of Frog design and led the company until 1999, when he cofounded Whipsaw, an engineering and industrial design consulting firm. Its diverse designs include emergency radios, retina scanners, and breast-shaped baby bottles. In 2009 Whipsaw was named one of "The Most Innovative Companies in Design" by *Fast Company* magazine. Harden has won over 150 design awards and has been granted over 200 design and utility patents. His work is in the permanent collections of the Cooper-Hewitt, National Design Museum in New York, the Chicago Athenaeum: Museum of Architecture and Design, and the Pasadena Museum of California Art. whipsaw.com

Goodwin Hartshorn was started in 2002 by Edward Goodwin and Richard Hartshorn following their studies in industrial design at London's Royal College of Art. Their multifaceted design work ranges from medical equipment, loudspeakers, and sanitaryware to furniture, consumer electronics, and domestic appliances. Projects include a compact tool kit for Brompton folding bicycles, easy-to-open food packaging for Waitrose grocery stores, and Child ViSion, which produces adjustable eyeglasses for children in the developing world. goodwin-hartshorn.co.uk

Stuart Haygarth (British, born 1966) graduated in 1988 from Exeter College of Art & Design with a bachelor's degree in graphic design and photography. He worked as a freelance designer and illustrator for many years, with clients such as Sony, Porsche, Penguin Books, and the British Broadcasting Corporation. In 2004 he began making things from his rich collection of found objects that most would consider trash. "My work is about giving banal and overlooked

objects a new significance". In 2007 Haygarth was named Best Breakthrough Designer by *Wallpaper* magazine and in 2008 he was awarded the New Designer Award by the *Elle Decor* British Design Awards. Haygarth has created several site-specific installations, most notably Framed, which was installed in a marble stairwell of the Victoria & Albert Museum during the 2010 London Design Festival. stuarthaygarth.com

Jaime Hayon (Spanish, born 1974) studied industrial design in Madrid and Paris. In 1997 he joined Fabrica, the Benetton-funded design and communication academy, where he was promoted from student to head of the Design Department. In 2004 Hayon started his own studio designing furniture, products, interiors, sculptures, and art installations, and now has offices in Italy, Spain, and the UK. His vision is rooted in a childhood obsession with graffiti and skateboard culture and straddles art, decoration, and design. Hayon's concern for the conservation of craft skills has led him to develop work for Baccarat, Bisazza, Established & Sons, Fabergé, Fritz Hansen, Lladró, and Magis, among others. He won the ELLE Deco International Award in 2006 and was named Designer of the Year at Now! Maison & Objet in 2010. hayonstudio.com

Hulger is a London-based boutique electronics company founded by Nicolas Roope and Michael-George Hemus in 2005. The company gained attention with its first product, a retro telephone handset that could be plugged into cell phones and computers. Their first model in production, the P*Phone, was launched in June 2005, and by the end of the year the company had sold over 10,000 units. In 2007 Hulger began work on the Plumen project with a goal to make a well-designed, appealing compact fluorescent lightbulb. The prototype, designed by Roope, is in the permanent collection of the Museum of Modern Art in New York. The Plumen 001, designed with Samuel Wilkinson, was released in 2001 and received the Brit Insurance Design of the Year Award and the Design & Art Direction Black Pencil Award. hulger.com

P*PHONE, HULGER

Giulio Iacchetti (Italian, born 1966) graduated from the architecture program at Politecnico di Milano and since 1992 has worked in the field of industrial design. In 2001 Moscardino, the multiuse biodegradable utensil he designed along with Matteo Ragni, won the Compasso d'Oro and became part of the permanent design collection of Museum of Modern Art in New York. In 2009 the Triennale Design Museum in Milan held a solo show of his work entitled *Giulio Iacchetti: Disobedient Objects*. giulioiacchetti.com

IMAC G3, JONATHAN IVE

Jonathan Ive (British, born 1967) holds a BA and an honorary doctorate from Newcastle Polytechnic. He cofounded the London-based studio Tangerine in the early 1990s. Apple hired his firm as a consultant and subsequently brought him to California to work full-time for the company. Within four years, Ive was promoted to senior vice president of industrial design. He worked closely with Apple's cofounder, Steve Jobs, to develop the iMac, the revolutionary computer that transformed the industry with its all-in-one design and bright colors, selling more than two million units in its first year. Following the iMac's launch, Ive was the lead designer for the iPod, iPhone, iPad, iPod Touch, MacBook Pro, and MacBook Air. In 2003, he was named Designer of the Year by the Design Museum in London and awarded the title Royal Designer for Industry by the British Royal Society of Arts. In 2012, he was knighted by the Order of the British Empire. apple.com

Kouji Iwasaki (Japanese, born 1965) joined the Nishimura Mashamitsu Design Studio in 1989. His To:Ca won first prize at the Asahikawa International Furniture Design Fair in 2002 and the iF Product Design Award in 2007.

Douwe Jacobs (Dutch, 1984) & Tom Schouten (Dutch, 1982) worked together on a concept for foldable, flat-pack furniture while students at Delft University of Technology. Following graduation in 2008, they started their own company with a small start-up loan from the university and created the prototype for their first design, the Flux chair. After winning the New Venture Award and the Philips Innovation Award in the Netherlands, Jacobs and Schouten used their prize money to further develop the Flux chair. In 2010, they paired with a team of entrepreneurs to help them make the Flux concept available internationally. fluxfurniture.com

Hella Jongerius (Dutch, born 1963) graduated from the Eindhoven Design Academy in 1993 and started her own company, Jongerius Lab. She also designed projects for Droog, the Dutch design collaborative. Her work fuses industry and craft, high and low technology, traditional and contemporary elements. She crosses boundaries of mass production by introducing imperfections and individuality into the industrial manufacturing process. Jongerius produces her own work and also creates for IKEA, Maharam, Royal Tichelaar Makkum, and Vitra. Her work has been shown at the Cooper-Hewitt, National Design Museum and the Museum of Modern Art in New York; the Design Museum in London; Galerie KREO in Paris; and Moss Gallery in New York. jongeriuslab.com

Patrick Jouin (French, born 1967) graduated from the École Nationale Supérieure de Création Industrielle in 1992. He subsequently worked for Thomson Multimedia and then joined the firm of Philippe Starck. In 1999, Jouin established his own studio for product design and interior architecture. His work is ubiquitous in France: ". . . on a typical day of walking around Paris, one encounters a Patrick Jouin design every 350 meters; he has contributed over 46,000 designs to the urban landscape."[9] His work in 3-D printing brought him international acclaim, as he was one of the first designers to use this technology for finished pieces rather than prototypes. Jouin has had solo exhibitions at the Centre Georges Pompidou in Paris and the Museum of Arts and Design in New York, and his work is in the permanent collections of the Museum of Modern Art and the Cooper-Hewitt, National Design Museum in New York. patrickjouin.com

SOLID C2 CHAIR, PATRICK JOUIN

Singgih S. Kartono (Indonesian, born 1968) graduated from Indonesia's Bandung Institute of Technology in 1992 with a degree in product design. Rather than remaining in the city and working for a design studio, he returned to his village of Kandangan in Central Java to help improve its economy and ecosystem. Kartono founded his company, Piranti Works, and taught workers carpentry skills. He also established a nursery, where trees are planted to replace those used in production; and he distributes young trees free to villagers to be replanted on their own land. Kartono's use of materials and his production methods are designed to help tackle the socioeconomic and ecological problems of his village. He received the Good Design Award in 2008. magno-design.com

Natalie Kruch (Canadian, born 1985) was a third-year under-graduate student at the University of Alberta when she designed the Balloona stool as part of a class assignment. After graduating in 2007, Natalie brought her prototype to the Toronto Interior Design Show, where it caught the eye of the manufacturer Umbra. The stool is now part of the permanent collection of the Philadelphia Museum of Art. Kruch has since enrolled in the architecture program at the University of British Columbia.

Tomáš Gabzdil Libertíny (Slovakian, born 1979) studied engineering and design at the Technical University Košice in Slovakia. In 2001 he received a scholarship to attend the University of Washington in Seattle, where he focused on painting and sculpture. He then enrolled in the master's program at the Design Academy Eindhoven, where he received his MFA in 2006. After graduation, Libertíny opened his design studio in Rotterdam. He has won several prestigious awards including Designer of the Future 2009 at Design Miami/Basel, a Dutch Design Award in 2009 and a Wallpaper* Design Award in 2010. His work is in the permanent collection of the Museum of Modern Art in New York, the Museum Boijmans van Beuningen, the Cincinnati Art Museum, and the Museum of Design and Contemporary Applied Arts in Lausanne. tomaslibertiny.com

Ross Lovegrove (British, born 1958) graduated from Manchester Polytechnic in 1980 and London's Royal College of Art in 1983. Following his graduation, he worked for Frog Design in Germany and on the development of Sony Walkman and Apple computers. He then consulted with major design and manufacturing companies before forming his own London-based practice, Studio X, in 1990. Lovegrove's work is inspired by the logic and beauty of nature, and his designs unite technology, materials, science, and the organic form. His work is included in the Museum of Modern Art in New York, the Design Museum in London, the Vitra Design Museum in Weil am Rhein, Germany, and many other institutions. rosslovegrove.com

Elena Manferdini (Italian, born 1974) graduated from the school of engineering at the Università di Bologna, and later received an M.Arch. from the University of California, Los Angeles. At her interdisciplinary design firm, Atelier Manferdini, founded in 2004, she applies a knowledge of engineering and construction to design products, clothing, and jewelry. A distinguishing characteristic of Manferdini's work, at every scale, is her use of patterning. She teaches at the Southern California Institute of Architecture in Los Angeles, and is a 2011 United States Artists, California Community Foundation Fellowship recipient. ateliermanferdini.com

Ingo Maurer (German, born 1932) studied graphic design in Munich and worked in the United States as a freelance designer until 1963. In 1966 he returned to Munich and opened his lighting studio. His first lamp was called Bulb and paid homage to his love of the bare lightbulb, which he has described as the perfect meeting of industry and poetry. It became an instant classic and was acquired by the Museum of Modern Art in New York. Maurer's career has spanned over fifty years and produced numerous lighting designs and technologies. A sculptor and inventor as well as a designer, he is known for transforming everyday materials into works of art. He has had solo exhibitions at the Cooper-Hewitt, National Design Museum in New York and the Philadelphia Museum of Art, and received the Compasso d'Oro Career Award in 2011. ingo-maurer.com

Yael Mer & Shay Alkalay (both Israeli, both born 1976) are founding partners of the London-based studio Raw-Edges. Since graduating from the Royal College of Art in 2006, they have received several highly respected awards, including The British Council Talented Award and a Designer of the Future Award from Design Miami/Basel (2009). Their work is in the Museum of Modern Art in New York, the Design Museum in London, and the Israel Museum in Jerusalem. Alkalay focuses on "turning two-dimensional sheet materials into curvaceous functional forms," while Mer "is fascinated by how things move, function and react." raw-edges.com

Issey Miyake (Japanese, born 1938) studied graphic design at Tama Art University in Tokyo. After graduating in 1964, he moved to Paris to study haute couture. Returning to Tokyo in 1970, he founded the Miyake Design Studio. The philosophy of his studio was to challenge preconceived ideas of design by combining traditional artisan techniques with the latest technologies. In 1998, Miyake began to develop A-POC (A Piece Of Cloth) with Dai Fujiwara. They used an industrial knitting and weaving machine programmed by a computer to transform a single thread into a complete piece of clothing, an accessory, or even a chair. Miyake's work has been exhibited worldwide, and A-POC is in the permanent collection of the

BULB LAMP, INGO MAURER

Museum of Modern Art in New York. Among his many awards is the Design of the Year in Fashion from London's Design Museum in 2012. mds.isseymiyake.com

Yoshitomo Nara (Japanese, born 1959) received a BFA and MFA from the Aichi Prefectural University of Fine Arts and Music in Japan in 1987. The following year, he moved to Germany, where he continued to study and paint for the next twelve years. By the time Nara returned to Japan in 2000, he had become a leader in the Japanese Neo Pop art movement. Citing rock and punk music as his greatest sources of inspiration, he developed a signature style,

depicting seemingly innocent children and animals with menacing undertones. Nara's work straddles the lines between fine art, illustration, and design, and can be found in galleries and museums as well as on T-shirts, ashtrays, skateboards, and postcards. narayoshitomo.com

New Deal Design is a creative agency founded in 2000 specializing in technology objects and information architecture. Based in San Francisco, the firm is led by founder Gadi Amit, former vice president of Frog Design. The firm has received over 100 design awards from IDEA, Red Dot Design Awards, *I.D.* Magazine, International Design Forum Hannover (iF), Good Design Award, and others, and their work has been exhibited in the Chicago Athenaeum, Cooper-Hewitt, National Design Museum, and the Museum of Modern Art in San Francisco. Their clients include start-ups like Lytro and Fitbit, as well as global brands such as Dell and Logitech. newdealdesign.com

Patrick Norguet (French, born 1969) studied engineering and industrial design, graduating from the École Nationale Supérieure de Création Industrielle in Paris in 1996. Three years later, he gained international attention for his Rainbow chair, which was later added to the permanent collections of the Museum of Modern Art in New York and the Philadelphia Museum of Art. Norguet's work is precise and elegant in its simplicity. He believes that "there is no place [in design] for the self-indulgent expression of the superego, ethereal concepts or media hype." Norguet received the *Wallpaper** Design Award for Best Domestic Design (2011) and the Red Dot Design Award (2010), and he was named Designer of the Year at Now! Maison & Objet in 2005. patricknorguet.com

APOLLO CHAIR, PATRICK NORGUET

Fabio Novembre (Italian, born 1966) received a degree in architecture from the Politecnico di Milano in 1992, and soon after opened his own studio. He has had a multifaceted career designing restaurants, discotheques, and shops, and on a smaller scale, furniture for Cappellini, Casamania, Driade, Flaminia, and Meritalia. His designs feature vibrant colors and curved, sensual lines, and as he has observed, "There's one exact thing that I've seen a million times and still remains the biggest inspiration of my work. The female body!"[10] In 2009 Novembre was invited to design his solo exhibition, *Il Fiore di Novembre*, at the Triennale Design Museum in Milan, and in 2012 at the same museum, he designed the exhibition *Grafica Italiana*. novembre.it

Shinichiro Ogata (Japanese, born 1969) is a designer of products, interiors, and graphics, as well as a restaurateur. He started his company, Simplicity, in 1998, with the goal of creating a "new type of modern Japanese culture."[11] His first restaurant, Higashi-Yama, was opened the year he founded Simplicity, and in 2004 he opened Higashiya, a traditional Japanese sweets shop, and Sabo, a tearoom by day, bar by night. He says, "'The design company and the restaurant co-exist. I run Higashi-Yama as if I'm inviting guests to my house, and the restaurant functions as a showroom for Simplicity as well."[12] In 2008 he became creative director of WASARA. The compostable tableware he designed won the gold prize and the grand prize in the 2009 Design for Asia (DFA) Awards as well as the 2010 Good Design Award from the Chicago Athenaeum.

Michele Oka Doner (American, born 1945) received a bachelor of science and design degree in 1966 and an MFA in 1968, both from the University of Michigan. As an artist-designer, her work crosses over from sculpture to furniture, jewelry, public art, and functional objects, all of it inspired by her lifelong study and appreciation of the natural world. Among her numerous public art installations, her best known is *A Walk on the Beach* at the Miami International Airport. Completed over a fifteen-year time span, the installation features 8,000 cast-bronze sea creatures, inlayed into a mile of terrazzo floor. Doner's work is in the permanent collections of the Metropolitan Museum of Art and the Cooper-Hewitt, National Design Museum in New York; the Art Institute of Chicago; and the Virginia Museum of Fine Arts in Richmond. micheleokadoner.com

Gaetano Pesce (Italian, born 1939) began his career as a fine artist, and in 1965 graduated with a degree in architecture from the University of Venice. His Up series of furniture, launched in 1969 by C & B Italia, brought him recognition as a leader in the

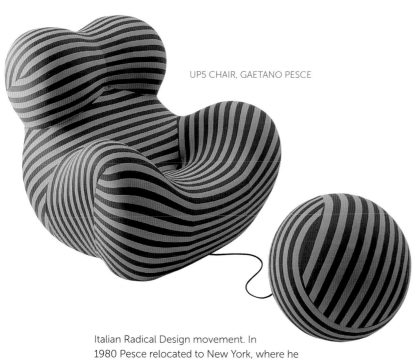

UP5 CHAIR, GAETANO PESCE

Italian Radical Design movement. In 1980 Pesce relocated to New York, where he has since worked in architecture, urban planning, interior design, industrial design, and publishing. One of his primary concerns has been the introduction of variability into the mass-production process, as his material of choice—liquid plastic resin—allows him to create similar but not identical objects, with variations in color, shape, and design. Pesce's work is in the permanent collections of the Museum of Modern Art and the Metropolitan Museum of Art in New York, the Victoria & Albert Museum in London, and the Centre Georges Pompidou in Paris. He received the Chrysler Award for Innovation and Design in 1993 and the Collab Design Excellence Award at the Philadelphia Museum of Art in 1995. gaetanopesce.com

Bertjan Pot (Dutch, born 1975) graduated from the Design Academy Eindhoven in 1998. He began work as a freelance designer, and in 2003 formed Studio Bertjan Pot. Relying on a high degree of handcrafting rather than industrial process, he experiments with new materials, sometimes spending years developing his techniques for their use. Pot's work is in the permanent collections of the Victoria & Albert Museum in London, the Stedelijk Museum Amsterdam, and the Museum of Modern Art in New York, among others. In 2012 he won the Frame Moooi Award. bertjanpot.nl

Matteo Ragni (Italian, born 1972) graduated with a degree in architecture from the Politecnico di Milano. As a child he was fascinated by the way things were made, so he took apart, rebuilt, and even reinvented new versions of household objects. In 2001 he was awarded the Compasso d'Oro for his unusual utensil, the disposable and biodegradable Moscardino spork, now in the permanent collection of the Museum of Modern Art in New York. Ragni is also a partner in the eyeglass company W-eye, where he designs hingeless, bentwood glasses handmade out of a variety of woods. matteoragni.com

Cédric Ragot (French, born 1973) graduated from the École Nationale Supérieure de Création Industrielle in 1999. In 2002 he founded his own firm, and designs in many different categories, including cosmetics, consumer electronics, tableware, sports equipment, furniture, and electrical appliances. He has no interest in specialization and prefers to experiment with new materials and processes. Ragot has worked with Cappellini, Häagen-Dazs, Panasonic, Rosenthal, and Swarovski. He received the Chicago Athenaeum Good Design Award for his Fast Vases (2009), and the Red Dot Design Award for his hand-mixer for Krups (2009) and his flat cables for Lacie (2012). cedricragot.com

Karim Rashid (Canadian, born Egypt, 1960) received a degree in industrial design from Carleton University in Ottawa, Canada, in 1982 and completed his postgraduate studies in Naples, Italy. Since the opening of his design practice in New York in 1993, he has completed nearly 4,000 design projects. Rashid's work is immediately recognizable by his signature curvilinear forms which he calls "blobjects" and bright, often pink, color palette. His philosophy rejects nostalgia, antiquated traditions, and references to the past, all of which he believes impede progress. The title of his book, *I Want to Change the World*, attests to his confidence in the power of design and his ability to use it. Rashid's work is in the permanent collections of more than twenty-two museums and is exhibited in galleries worldwide. He has received the Red Dot Design Award, the Chicago Athenaeum Good Design Award, and the Industrial Designers Society of America Design Excellence Award, and has been cited by the *I.D.* Magazine Annual Design Review. karimrashid.com

METHOD DISH SOAP, KARIM RASHID

Jaime Salm (Colombian, born 1978) received a bachelor's degree in industrial design from the University of the Arts in Philadelphia in 2001. Following graduation, with his brother Isaac he cofounded MIO, a sustainable design company. The firm's mission is to create what they call "green desire"—consumers craving products that are sustainable and responsible. They work exclusively with renewable and recyclable materials and use manufacturers with sustainable practices. In 2009 Salm designed an eco-friendly outdoor living collection for Target. The firm received the Best Collection Award at the New York International Gift Fair in 2005. MIO's PaperForm wall tiles are in the permanent collection of the Cooper-Hewitt, National Design Museum in New York. mioculture.com

Marijn van der Poll (Dutch, born 1973) graduated from the Design Academy Eindhoven in 2002. While in school, he designed the Do Hit chair, which was later produced by Droog Design. He began his design studio while still a student and specialized in furniture and mobility design. A lover of cars, van der Poll designed and built several unique cars for both himself and Marcel Wanders. His most well known vehicle is the CM426 Merlin, which has a stainless steel open-top body and can occasionally be seen on Dutch roads, piloted by the designer. Van der Poll's work has been exhibited in museums and galleries around the world, including Traffic in Dubai and the Louvre in Paris, and is included in the permanent collection of the Victoria & Albert Museum in London. marijnvanderpoll.com

Dirk Vander Kooij (Dutch, born 1983) graduated from the Design Academy Eindhoven in 2010. His thesis project addressed the limitations of 3-D printing for large-scale objects. Vander Kooij developed his own printing technique using a robot that extrudes recycled plastic. He created the Endless Chair using this process, gaining him worldwide attention. The chair was acquired by the Museum of Modern Art in New York, the Stedelijk Museum in Amsterdam, and the Vitra Design Museum in Germany. In 2011, he was awarded a prestigious Dutch Design Award. In 2013 Vander Kooij exhibited at the International Contemporary Furniture Fair, where he was given the Editors Award for New Designer. dirkvanderkooij.nl

Diederik Schneemann (Dutch, born 1979) studied at the AKI Academy of Fine Arts and Design in Enschede, Netherlands. After graduation, he founded Studio Schneemann in Rotterdam. Schneemann first gained attention in 2011, when he presented his Flip Flop Story at the Salone di Mobile in Milan. In 2013, he exhibited again with Mash-Up, a series of objects composed of the rearranged parts of design classics. The work is homage to Schneemann's favorite designers, and confronts copyright and ownership of design issues that are emerging along side the fast growing 3-D printing industry. studioschneeman.com

Kurt Solland (American, born 1963) grew up surrounded by craftsmen and has been designing and inventing products since the age of eleven. In 1990 he received a bachelor's degree in industrial design from the University of Washington. As vice president of industrial design at Harman Consumer Group, he directed the design vision for products by Harman Kardon, Infinity, and JBL. Combining his passions for music and sculpture, Solland brought personality and innovation to desktop speakers, which previously had been plain, dull boxes. He has also independently designed and licensed a line of bicycle components, fitness products, LED lighting, and jewelry, and holds over 95 patents. In 2011 Solland joined Lenovo as Vice President of Design for its Mobile Internet and Digital Home Business Group, where he is responsible for positioning their entire product line of computers, laptops, tablets, and smartphones.

MAX HEATER, MATTI WALKER

Matti Walker (Swiss, born 1966) began his studies in painting and later apprenticed as a graphic designer for an advertising agency. He completed his education at the Color Psychology Institute, founded by Heinrich Frieling. In 1991 Walker opened his own graphic design firm, Atelier Farbton, located in a small village in the Swiss Alps. He began his long partnership with Stadler Form in 1999 when the firm hired him to design its first product, the Fred humidifier. The success of Fred, with its playful design and graphic colors, led Walker to design eight more products for the company: Max, Charly, Henry, Lilly, Oskar, Anton, Albert, and Anna. In 2008 Fred was featured in the exhibition *Design & Emotion* at the Badisches Landesmuseum in Karlsruhe, Germany. The Max heater received the Accent on Design Award at the New York International Gift Fair in 2002, and Anna, a ceramic heater, was awarded the Gold Medal for overall winner at the International Home & Housewares Show in Chicago in 2012.

Marcel Wanders (Dutch, born 1963) graduated from the ArtEZ Hogeschool voor de Kunsten in 1988. In 1995 he opened his own studio in Amsterdam and first gained attention when he created the Knotted Chair for Droog Design. Wanders infuses romanticism and a sense of history into his work, whether it's a vase, chandelier, bathtub, or hotel interior: "I want to make work that looks to the future, but also back to the past. I want to use new techniques, but also reintroduce that lost quality of beauty."[13] In 2008 he was featured on the cover of *Fast Company's* issue titled "Masters of Design," and in 2011 the *New York Times* called him the Lady Gaga of the design world.[14] Wanders' work is in the collections of the Museum of Modern Art in New York and the Museum of Modern Art in San Francisco, the Victoria & Albert Museum in London, and the Stedelijk Museum Amsterdam, among others. Wanders was named Designer of the Year by the ELLE Decoration International Design Awards in 2006, and received the Collab Design Excellence Award at the Philadelphia Museum of Art in 2009. marcelwanders.com

Samuel Wilkinson (British, born 1977) graduated from Ravensbourne College of Art & Design in London in 2002. He then spent five years working for design consultancies, with clients such as Audi, British Airways, LG, and Samsung. In 2007 he established his studio in East London. Wilkinson collaborated with the design company Hulger on the Plumen 001 lightbulb, which in 2011 was named the Design of the Year by London's Design Museum. That same year it also received the Black Pencil Award for Product Design from D&AD (Bristish Design & Art Direction). The Plumen 001 is in the permanent collections of the Victoria & Albert Museum in London and the Cooper-Hewitt, National Design Museum in New York. samuelwilkinson.com

Richard Woods (British, born 1966) graduated from the Winchester School of Art in 1988 and the Slade School of Fine Art, University College London in 1990. His signature Pop art aesthetic bridges the boundaries between art, architecture, and design. Woods uses traditional woodblock printing techniques to exaggerate elements of British architecture, such as Tudor beams, wood grain, brick, and stone. His art covers walls, floors, and entire buildings. In 2007, Woods began a collaboration with designer Sebastian Wrong on a collection of furniture for Established & Sons. Woods's work has been exhibited in museums and galleries worldwide, including the Serpentine Gallery and the Victoria & Albert Museum in London. richardwoodsstudio.com

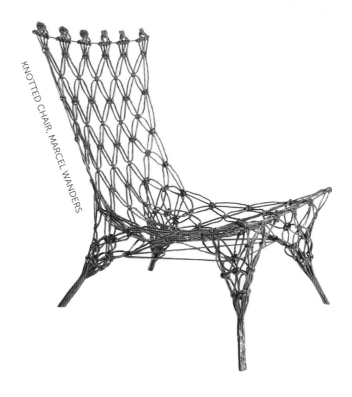

KNOTTED CHAIR, MARCEL WANDERS

Sebastian Wrong (British, born 1971) studied sculpture at the Norwich School of Art and Design and graduated in 1993 from the Camberwell School of Art and Crafts in London. In 1995 he founded his own manufacturing company and began to develop a strong technical expertise in production. In 2005 he cofounded and became design director of Established & Sons. Wrong's experience in manufacturing and emphasis on innovation contributes to the firm's complex designs. In 2007 he co-created the Wrongwoods collection with artist Richard Woods. Wrong designed the deceptively simple furniture, and Woods created the surface treatments. In 2002 Wrong received a Red Dot Design Award for his Spun lamp, produced by Flos, and in 2007 his Font Clock was exhibited at the aA Design Museum in Seoul. establishedandsons.com

Tony Wurman (American, born 1973) trained as an industrial designer and a glass blower. He was the creative director of a medical imaging company before founding Wunderwurks Design in New York. His chosen medium, a blend of EVA adhesive (hot glue), and his proprietary techniques produce objects with the qualities of glass but with the flexibility of rubber. "If they succeed, the result can be a Venini- or Tiffany- or Chihuly-style object that can be drop-kicked across the room."[15] Wurman's fascination with the complexities of biological structures can be seen in the intricate patterns he creates, and his vast range of products includes lamps, vases, bowls, and jewelry. wunderwurks.com

Tokujin Yoshioka (Japanese, born 1967) graduated from Tokyo's Kuwasawa Design School in 1986. He worked for Shiro Kuramata and Issey Miyake before setting up his own studio in 2000. At the 2002 Milan Furniture Fair, Yoshioka released his now famous Honey-Pop chair, made of expandable honeycomb paper: His work is often described as ethereal, and Issey Miyake has remarked, "I believe that he is at his best when he makes skillful use of air, light, and sometimes even gravity."[16] Yoshioka's aim is to evoke emotion and speak to the senses, but experimentation with materials and technology is also a driving force in his work, as in his Second Nature chair, grown from crystals in a transparent tank. In 2007 he received the Designer of the Year Award at Design Miami, and in 2010 he was named one of the "100 Most Creative People in Business" by *Fast Company* magazine. His work is in the Museum of Modern Art and the Cooper-Hewitt, National Design Museum in New York; the Centre Georges Pompidou in Paris; the Victoria & Albert Museum in London; and the Vitra Design Museum in Weil am Rhein, Germany. tokujin.com

Oskar Zieta (Polish, born 1975) studied architecture before pursuing a PhD in computer-aided architectural design at the Eidgenössische Technische Hochschule Zürich (ETH), where he now teaches. His thesis research led to the development of FiDU (Free Inner Pressure Deformation), a process of inflating sheet metal into lightweight and sturdy objects that can be transported flat: "Before they are inflated 100 of my [Plopp] stools will fit on a pallet, although if they were all blown up they would fill up a container."[17] In 2007 he founded his design company, Zieta Prozessdesign, as well as the manufacturing company Steelwerk Polska, which produces his line of inflated steel furniture and objects. Zieta has continued to research the applications of FiDU, and in 2008 built a footbridge with his students at ETH that could withstand over 4,000 pounds of weight—demonstrating its potential use in architecture and engineering. Zieta won the Red Dot Design Award for his Plopp stool in 2008, and the German Design Council's Young Professional of the Year Award in 2009. In 2011 he was given the Audi Mentor Prize by *A&W* magazine. His work can be found in the permanent collections of the Centre Georges Pompidou in Paris, the Museum für Gestaltung Zürich, and the Pinakothek der Modern in Munich. zieta.pl

PLOPP STOOL, OSKAR ZIETA

Pamela Zonsius (American, born 1952) received a bachelor of fashion design degree from the Fashion Institute of Technology in Los Angeles. She spent the first part of her career as an award-winning designer in the fashion industry. In 2005, she switched gears when she invented the Brelli, the worlds first 100 percent biodegradable umbrella. In 2009, Zonsius was awarded the Material Vision Design Plus Award for the Brelli and in 2011 was nominated for the Design Award of the Federal Republic of Germany. thebrelli.com

1. Yves Behar, foreword to *Material Change: Design Thinking and the Social Entrepreneurship Movement*, by Eve Blossom (New York: D.A.P./Distributed Art Publishers, 2011), p. 6.

2. designmuseum.org/design/ronan-erwan-bouroullec.

3. designmuseum.org/design/ronan-erwan-bouroullec.

4. core77.com/blog/ny_design_week/ny_design_week_2012_preview_wanteddesign_qa_with_francois_brument_22465.asp.

5. Charlotte Fiell and Peter Fiell, *Design Now!* (Cologne: Taschen, 2007), p. 146.

6. Quoted at www.normann-copenhagen.com.

7. *Dwell* magazine online interview conducted in September 2006.

8. Interview by the author, 6.14.12.

9. mgxbymaterialise.com.

10. Quoted at nowness.com 3.21.12.

11. Wilson, Fiona. "Tea and Simplicity," *Wallpaper*, 10.04: 140–14.

12. Wilson, Fiona. "Tea and Simplicity," *Wallpaper*, 10.04: 140–14.

13. dwell.com/articles/profiles-marcel-wanders.

14. Julie Scelfo, "Marcel Wanders on Designing Upbeat Tableware," *New York Times*, 3.16.11.

15. David A. Keeps, "Icons of the Garden," *Los Angeles Times*, 9.21.06.

16. Ryu Niimi, *Tokujin Yoshioka Design* (London: Phaidon, 2006), p. 10.

17. Interview by Nora Schmidt, architonic.com/ntsht/blow-up-sheet-metal/7000205.

The urge for good design is the same as the urge to go on living.

Harry Bertoia

shop

Alessi
alessi-shop.com
Online shopping for everything Alessi for the kitchen, bath, and home.

Bobby Berk Home
bobbyberkhome.com
Bobby Berk Home carries all you need to furnish a modern lifestyle. Stores in New York and Miami.

Cooper-Hewitt Shop
shop.cooperhewitt.org
Gift shop of the Smithsonian's Cooper-Hewitt, National Design Museum, offering a broad range of design books and a uniquely curated selection of goods from around the globe.

Design Public
designpublic.com
Hip and accessible shop for everything from affordable gifts to high-end furniture.

Design Within Reach
dwr.com
One of the first companies to introduce the public to modern furniture traditionally found only in designer showrooms. A resource for modern, contemporary, and unique furniture and accessories. Online, print catalog, and showroom sales.

Fab
fab.com
Curated online shop featuring products from up-and-comers and design stars, as well as their own Fab-branded designs.

Fitzsu Society
fitzsu.com
Designer home accessories store located in Los Angeles, with a website that offers detailed product information and a registry service.

The Future Perfect
shop.thefutureperfect.com
New York City–based store featuring the work of designers on the forefront of contemporary design.

Hive Modern
hivemodern.com
Home furnishing and accessories shop, carrying brands from Alessi to Vitra. Website and storefront in Portland, Oregon.

Luminaire
luminaire.com
This pioneering force in the design world has reshaped the idea of what a design store can be for over 38 years. Stores located in Chicago, Miami, and Coral Gables, or shop online.

Matter
mattermatters.com
New York–based contemporary design store and manufacturer featuring furniture, lighting, wallpaper, home accessories, and their own collection, Mattermade.

MoMA Store
momastore.org
A wide selection of products—reviewed by curators at the Museum of Modern Art in New York—reflecting the latest materials, production techniques, and design concepts. Includes designs that are in the museum's permanent collection.

mossPOP
mosspop.com
Murray Moss and Franklin Getchell opened this online shop after closing their well-known SoHo design gallery, Moss. Includes a highly curated selection of unusual objects, furniture, and jewelry with prices ranging from $20 to $90,000.

Muji
muji.us/store
Online shop and retail locations featuring furniture, clothing, and home accessories, all in Muji's signature no-brand style.

Nova 68
nova68.com
Fine modern design with a large selection of contemporary lighting, home accessories, books, and classic toys from Europe.

Stardust
stardust.com
Thousands of modern and contemporary design furniture, lighting, and home accessories. Retail store located in Sonoma, California.

Surrounding
surrounding.com
Specializes in contemporary lighting from around the world.

SwitchModern
switchmodern.com
Atlanta-based showroom turned webshop, carrying everything for the home from dog bowls to dining room tables.

Unica Home
unicahome.com
One of the largest selections of modern design, furnishings, lighting, and accessories, including many pieces that cannot be purchased anywhere else in the United States.

YLiving
yliving.com
Well-edited collection of furniture and accessories, from mid-century modern to cutting-edge contemporary.

read

Azure
azuremagazine.com
Toronto-based print magazine and blog that profiles international designers and architects, reports on major trade fairs, and explores design issues related to our changing society.

Core 77
core77.com
Reports and reviews the latest news and events in the design world. Includes extensive resources for designers, from job and portfolio boards to comprehensive lists of design firms and design schools.

Designboom
designboom.com
Founded in 1999, Designboom was the first online design and architecture magazine. Publishes the latest news and reports on key issues in all aspects of design, architecture, and art.

Design Milk
design-milk.com
Design blog focusing on the latest in contemporary art, furniture, architecture, interior design, style, technology, and home accessories.

Design Observer
designobserver.com
News and critical essays on design, urbanism, social innovation, and popular culture by leading design thinkers and writers.

Design*Sponge
designsponge.com
Design and lifestyle blog including home tours, DIY projects, "before and after" projects, city guides, and shopping guides.

Dezeen
dezeen.com
Online magazine that presents a selection of architecture, design, and interiors from around the world.

Dwell
dwell.com
Comprehensive design resource featuring home tours, product guides, travel tips, and interviews with the world's design leaders.

Fast Company
fastcodesign.com
Magazine and blog with an editorial focus on business, innovation in technology, ethonomics (ethical economics), leadership, and design.

Sight Unseen
sightunseen.com
Behind-the-scenes peek into the lives and studios of creative leaders.

Moco Loco
mocoloco.com
Daily design guide dedicated to modern contemporary design and architecture.

Metropolis
metropolismag.com
Print magazine and daily blog that examine contemporary life through design: architecture, interior design, product design, graphic design, crafts, planning, and preservation.

Yatzer
yatzer.com
News, interviews, and reviews covering design, architecture, travel, art, fashion, and events.

notes

All websites were active at the time of publication, unless otherwise indicated.

CHAPTER 1: MATERIALITY

Peacock Chair: Dror Benshetrit, interview by the author, 10.21.11.
Zeppelin: Marcel Wanders, interview by the author, 3.2.11.
Blow Up Bamboo Centerpiece: *The Campana Brothers: Complete Works (So Far)* (New York: Rizzoli, 2010), 122; Fernando Campana and Humberto Campana, interview with the author, 2.17.11.
Midsummer Light: Linda Hales, "The Flowering of Tord Boontje," *Washington Post,* 2.12.05, C02; Tord Boontje, interview by the author, 3.6.11.
Osorom Bench: Moroso, interview by the author, 2.13.07; Laurel Saville and Brooke Stoddard, *Design Secrets: Furniture: 50 Real-Life Projects Uncovered* (Gloucester, Mass.: Rockport, 2006), 703; product description by Konstantin Grcic Industrial Design, konstantingrcic. com.
Samurai Lamp: Ingo Maurer, introduction to *The MaMo Nouchies: A New Tribe of Light* (Munich: Ingo Maurer, 1998); Michael Webb, *Ingo Maurer,* Compact Design Portfolio Series (San Francisco: Chronicle Books, 2003), 11.
Carbon Chair: product description by Studio Bertjan Pot, bertjanpot.nl; product description by International Council of Societies of Industrial Design, 5.20.08, icsid.org; Kristi Cameron, "It's Elemental," *Metropolis,* 6.1.04, metropolismag.com.

CHAPTER 2: PROCESS

Smoke Dining Chair: Kristi Cameron, "Why Maarten Baas Burns through History," *Metropolis,* 4.25.04, metropolismag.com; Marcus Fairs, *21st Century Design: New Design Icons from Mass Market to Avant-Garde* (London: Carlton, 2006), 150–51; Linda Hales, "Maarten Baas's Claims to Flame," *Washington Post,* 5.22.04., C02.
Vase of Phases: Dror Benshetrit, interview by the author, 2.18.11; Cator Sparks, "Top Dror," *City Magazine,* Summer 2007: 46.
Chippensteel Chair: Monica Khemsurov, "Oskar Zieta's Metal-Inflating Facility," *Sight Unseen,* 12.14.10, sightunseen.com; Nora Schmidt, "Blow Up Sheet Metal," *Architonic,* n.d., architonic.com; Riya Patel, "Oskar Zieta," *ICON,* no. 096, 7.11: 65.
Bin Bin: John Brauer, interview by the author, 1.24.11.
One Shot Stool: Patrick Jouin, interview by the author, 2.17.11.
Random Light: product description by Moooi, moooi.com.
Illusion Side Table: John Brauer, interview by the author, 1.24.11.
Blossom: product description by Atelier Manferdini, ateliermanferdini.com; Elena Manferdini, interview by the author, 9.20.11.
Bank in the Form of a Pig: Harry Allen, interview by the author, 1.14.11.

CHAPTER 3: DESIGN FOR TECHNOLOGY

Looksoflat Lamp: "Stefan Geisbauer: Look So Flat for Ingo Maurer," *Designboom,* 4.18.11, designboom.com.

CHAPTER 4: SHAPE SHIFTERS

Fast Vase: Cedric Ragot, interview by the author, 1.19.11.
Fred Humidifier: Stadler Form, interview by the author, 1.10.11.
Stack: Teri Peters, "Designer Identity: Raw Edges," *Azure* 6.09: 44–46; Jordan Kushins, "Q&A with Sebastian Wrong," *Dwell,* 4.6.09, dwell.com.
Collapsible Strainer: profile of Boje Estermann by manufacturer Normann Copenhagen, normann-copenhagen.com; Boje Estermann, interview by the author, 1.9.11.
Mercury Ceiling Light: Peter Hall, "Ross Lovegrove's New Series for Artemide," *Metropolis* 5.09: 101–5.

CHAPTER 5: VARIANCE

Nobody's Perfect Chair: Eils Lotozo, "If Looks Could Liberate," *Philadelphia Inquirer,* 11.18.05: e1+.
Algues: Product description by Ronan and Erwan Bouroullec, bouroullec.com.
IO Vase: Tony Wurman, interview by the author, 8.16.12.
To be continued: "2 (Or 3 . . .) Questions for Julien Carretero," *MocoLoco,* 8.6.09, mocoloco.com; product description by Moss Gallery, moss-gallery.com (site no longer active).
Airborne Snotty Vase: Marcel Wanders, interview by the author, 2.17.11.

CHAPTER 6: BLURRING THE LINES

WrongWoods Sideboard: Virginia Gardiner, "Wrong Woods," *Dwell,* 1.1.09, dwell.com.
Ripple Chair + A-Poc Gemini Vest: Reena Jana, "Case Study: Issey Miyake, The Dream Weaver," *Bloomberg BusinessWeek,* 4.25.06, businessweek.com.
Love Bowl: Product description by Readymade Projects, readymadeprojects.com; Monica Khemsurov, "Worldly Goods," *T Magazine, New York Times,* 9.28.08, newyorktimes.com.
Rados: Michele Oka Doner, interview by the author, 1.8.11.
Zig Zag Shoes and Bag: Fernando Campana and Humberto Campana, interview by the author, 1.28.11.
Balloona Stool: Natalie Kruch, interview by the author, 2.17.11.

CHAPTER 7: SUSTAINABILITY

Moscardino Spork: Collin Dunn, "Moscardino Spork," *Treehugger*, 7.26.05, treehugger.com.
Brelli: Pam Zonsius, interview by the author, 1.10.11.
Plumen: "Plumen 001," in *Brit Insurance Designs of the Year*, ed. Anna Faherty, 176–77, exh. cat. (Design Museum, London, 2011); Marcus Fairs, "Plumen Low-Energy Bulbs by Hulger," *Dezeen*, 11.21.07, dezeen.com.
Bobble: Karim Rashid, interview by the author, 1.11.11.

CHAPTER 8: DESIGN FOR GOOD

NYC Condom Dispenser and Wrapper: Yves Béhar, interview by the author, 6.7.11; case study by Fuseproject, fuseproject.com.
XO Laptop: CV for Yves Béhar, Fuseproject, fuseproject.com.
Johnson & Johnson First Aid Kit: Harry Allen, interview by the author, 1.20.11; product description by Harry Allen design, harryallendesign.com.
Height-Adjustable Tub Rail: John Hockenberry, "The Re-Education of Michael Graves", *Metropolis*, October 2006, metropolismag.com.
Home Hero: Jon Wilde, "The iPod of Fire Extinguishers: Home Depot Home Hero," *Men's Journal*, 10.08, mensjournal.com.
See Better to Learn Better: Jacob Slevin, "Designer Yves Béhar Helps Children of Mexico See Better," *Huffington Post*, 8.30.11, huffingtonpost.com.

bibliography

Alessi, Alberto. *Alessi: The Design Factory*. 2nd ed. London: Academy, 1998.
Bauer, Helmut, ed. *Ingo Maurer: Making Light*. Munich: Nazraeli, 1992.
Böhm, Florian, ed. *KGID: Konstantin Grcic Industrial Design*. London: Phaidon, 2005.
Byars, Mel. *The Design Encyclopedia*. London: Laurence King Publishing; New York: The Museum of Modern Art, 2004.
Campana, Humberto, Fernando Campana, et al. *The Campana Brothers: Complete Works (So Far)*. New York: Rizzoli, 2010.
Dixon, Tom, et al. *& Fork*. London: Phaidon, 2007.
Fairs, Marcus. *21st Century Design*. London: Carlton, 2009.
Fiell, Charlotte, and Peter Fiell. *Design Now!* Cologne: Taschen, 2007.
Guillaume, Valérie. *Patrick Jouin*. Exh. cat., Centre Pompidou, Galerie du Musée. Paris: Éditions du Centre Pompidou, 2010.
Lovell, Sophie. *Furnish: Furniture and Interior Design for the 21st Century*. Berlin: Die Gestalten Verlag, 2007.
Margetts, Martina, et al. *Tord Boontje*. New York: Rizzoli, 2006.
Niimi, Ryu, et al. *Tokujin Yoshioka Design*. London: Phaidon, 2006.
Polster, Bernard, et al. *The A–Z of Modern Design*. Rev. and updated ed. London: Merrell, 2009.
Rashid, Karim. *I Want to Change the World*. New York: Universe, 2001.
Schouwenberg, Louise, ed. *Hella Jongerius: Misfit*. London: Phaidon, 2010.
Starck, Philippe, et al. *Starck*. Cologne: Taschen, 2003.

photo credits

All photography by Kelly Turso except the following images:

INTRODUCTION TIMELINE
85 Lamps for Droog by Rody Graumans—Gerard van Hees/www.droog.com

MATERIALITY
Honey-Pop Chair—Courtesy Tokujin Yoshioka

PROCESS
Him & Her Chairs—Casamania
Chubby Chair—Dirk Vander Kooij

DESIGN FOR TECHNOLOGY
Amiigo—Courtesy Amiigo
CubeX Trio—3D Systems Corporation

VARIANCE
To be continued—Courtesy Moss Bureau
Do hit Chair—Marijn van der Poll/Droog

BLURRING THE LINES
The Honeycomb Vase—Raoul Kramer

SUSTAINABILITY
Tide Chandelier—Stuart Haygarth
Kaktus—Location courtesy Terrain, Glen Mills, Pennsylvania
Plumen—Ian Nolan © HULGER
Flip Flop Vase—Martin Minkenberg

Bio A–Z
Banana Bowl—Areaware
SAYL Chair—Courtesy Herman Miller, Inc.
QuaDror—Dror, Inc.
Sushi Chair III—Courtesy Moss Bureau
Chair One—Tom Vack
Adiri Baby Bottle—WHIPSAW INC.
Showtime Vases—BD Barcelona Design
P*Phone—Tony Summerskill © HULGER
Solid C2 Chair—Thomas Duval
Apollo Chair—Studio Norguet Design
Up5 Chair—B&B Italia
Mash-Up Chair—Martin Minkenberg
Endless Pulse Low Chair—Dirk Vander Kooij
Plopp Stool—Courtesy Zieta Prozessdesign

acknowledgments

Thank you Caroline Tiger for your incredible contribution to the content of this book; Maria Eife for your intelligent research assistance; Kelly Turso for your endless creative photography; Lisa Benn for staying sane through the graphic design process; Ron Broadhurst and Mary Cason for your insightful editing.

And thank you to all the people who, like me, just can't get enough of great design.

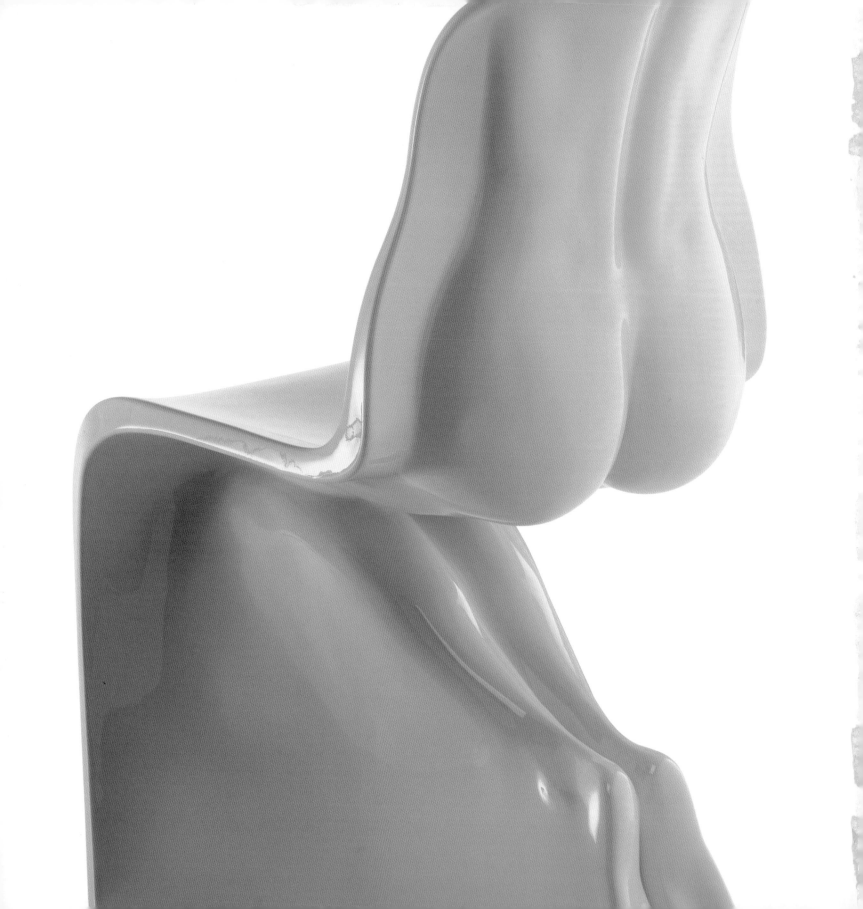